Workbook

Business Math

SIXTEENTH EDITION

Robert A. Schultheis

Raymond M. Kaczmarski

Australia · Brazil · Canada · Mexico · Singapore · Spain · United Kingdom · United States

**Workbook
Business Math, 16ᵗʰ Edition**

Robert A. Schultheis and Raymond M. Kaczmarski

VP/Editorial Director
Jack W. Calhoun

VP/Editor-in-Chief
Karen Schmohe

VP/Educational Marketing
Carol Volz

Executive Editor
Eve Lewis

Project Manager
Enid Nagel

Marketing Manager
Nancy Long

Ancillary Coordinator
Kelly Resch

Editorial Assistant
Linda Keith

Manufacturing Coordinator
Kevin Kluck

Art Director
Stacy Jenkins Shirley

Cover Designer
Beckmeyer Design, Inc.

Cover Image(s)
© Getty Images

Printer
Darby Printing Company
Atlanta, GA

Table of Contents

This page intentionally blank.

Lesson 1.1 *Hourly Pay and Salary*

Exercises

1. Vladimir Hirsch worked these hours last week: Monday, 8 hours; Tuesday, 7 hours; Wednesday, 5 hours; Thursday, 5 hours; Friday, 7 hours. He is paid $16 an hour. **a.** How many hours did Vladimir work last week? **b.** What was his gross pay for the week?

2. Elvera Hulon earns $12 an hour at her job. The hours she worked during each of the last four weeks are shown below. For each week find the gross pay Elvera earned. Then find her total gross pay for four weeks. Write your answers in the chart.

Week	Hours Worked	Gross Pay
1	38	
2	40	
3	31	
4	37	
	Total Gross Pay	

3. Jackie Bradford has two jobs. Her full-time job pays $15 an hour. A part-time job pays $8 an hour. Last week Jackie worked 35 hours at her full-time job and 17 hours at her part-time job. **a.** Find the gross pay she earned at her full-time job. **b.** Find the gross pay she earned at her part-time job. **c.** Find the total amount she earned from both jobs

4. Padraig Wright earns a weekly salary of $465. **a.** How much would Padraig earn in 4 weeks of work? **b.** How much would he earn in a 52-week year?

5. Wanda Dougherty earned a weekly salary of $509 for the first 26 weeks of the year. She changed jobs and was paid a weekly salary of $576 for the last 26 weeks of the year. What total gross pay did Wanda earn for the year?

     Chapter 1 *Workbook*

Lesson 1.2 *Average Pay*

Exercises

1. Josh Duchene worked at three jobs in three weeks. In the first week, he earned $360. In the next week, he was paid $345. In the third week, he was paid $315. What average pay per week did Josh earn for these three weeks?

2. The monthly earnings of Elisa Harrington for July through October were: $2,087; $1,912; $1,876; $2,005. What average amount per month did she earn for these four months?

3. Sherman Cole worked five days last week and earned these amounts: $95.04, $88.42, $83.97, $96.31, $103.49. What average amount per day did Sherman earn during these five days, rounded to the nearest cent?

4. Elisa Beaufait has worked as a health spa manager for the past three years. During her first year, she earned $37,340. Her earnings increased to $38,754 the second year, and to $41,920 the third year. What were her average annual earnings for the three years she worked for the spa?

5. Five part-time workers at Lou's Diner earned gross pay last week of $95.10, $76.23, $77.39, $89.30, and $105.46. What was the average gross pay of these workers, rounded to the nearest cent?

6. Ian Zander earns extra money by refinishing wood floors. His charge is based on the size and condition of the floor. Last month, he refinished 6 floors for $140 each, 2 floors for $220 each and 1 floor for $178. What average amount per floor did he earn for the month?

Lesson 1.2 *Average Pay*

7. After working at her new job, Mabel Ridgeway found that she had earned the following monthly salaries: $2,400 monthly for the first 3 months; $2,650 monthly for the following 2 months; $2,830 for the sixth month. What average amount per month did Mabel earn during these six months?

8. Four employees of Borden Testing Labs earn $18 an hour. Another 6 employees earn $23 an hour, while 4 others are paid $13 an hour. What is the average pay per hour earned by the employees, to the nearest cent?

9. Lynwood Bauer was paid $7.25 an hour for his first two months of work at his after-school job. He earned $7.45 an hour in the next month and $7.75 for the next 4 months. What was his average hourly pay rate for the months he worked at his part-time job, to the nearest cent?

10. By working for 4 weeks at your part-time job you earned these amounts: $126, $84, $105, $112. What pay will you have to earn in the fifth week to average $110 a week for five weeks **of** work?

11. The average weekly pay of five employees of Fairside Home Furnishings is $853. The weekly pay of four of the employees is $760, $911, $817, $795. What is the weekly pay of the other employee?

12. On Wednesday, five employees of the Wilson Tile Company earned an average gross pay of $136 for the day. Four of the employees earned these amounts on that day: $138, $127, $139, $151. How much did the fifth employee earn on Wednesday?

Lesson 1.3 *Regular and Overtime Pay*

Exercises

1. Jerrold Rogers is paid $10.40 an hour for regular-time work. **a.** What is Jerrold's time-and-a-half pay rate an hour? **b.** What is his double-time pay rate an hour?

2. Jadwiga Skowron worked 9 hours at time-and-a-half pay. Her regular-pay rate was $14.54 an hour. What was Jadwiga's total overtime pay?

3. On a weekend, Neville Hagberg worked 13 hours at double-time pay. His regular-pay rate was $9.86. What did Neville's overtime pay for the weekend total?

4. Last week, Wendy Pell earned $440 for regular-time work by working 40 regular-time hours at $11 an hour. For the week, she was also paid time-and-a-half pay for 7 overtime hours and double-time pay for another $6\frac{1}{2}$ hours. What were her total earnings for the week?

5. Drake Kennedy's regular-time pay rate is $12.73 an hour. Last week he was paid for 37.5 hours at his regular rate and for 5 hours at a time-and-a-half overtime rate. Find Drake's gross pay for the week.

6. Barbara Cusumano worked 60 hours last week. Of those hours, 40 hours were paid at the regular-time rate of $12.50 an hour, 18 hours at the time-and-a-half rate, and 2 hours at the double-time rate. What was Barbara's gross pay for the week?

  Chapter 1 *Workbook*

Lesson 1.3 *Regular and Overtime Pay*

7. Irving Manz works for Ben's Food Mart. He is paid weekly on the basis of a 40-hour week at the rate of $8.95 an hour with time-and-a-half for overtime. During one week he works $49\frac{1}{2}$ hours. What was the amount of his total earnings for the week?

8. The Sunlite Window Company's regular workweek is 8 hours a day, Monday through Friday. Workers get time-and-a-half for work over 8 hours per day. Carrie Wallis works for Sunlite and is paid a regular hourly rate of $13.76. One week she worked these hours: Monday, 8; Tuesday, $8\frac{3}{4}$; Wednesday, 9; Thursday, 10; Friday, $9\frac{1}{2}$. **a.** During the week how many regular hours did Carrie work? **b.** During the week how many overtime hours did Carrie work? **c.** What were her total earnings for the week?

9. Stefan Edward's pay is figured weekly, but is paid every two weeks. His pay is based on a 40-hour week at a regular-pay rate of $12.07 an hour with time-and-a-half for overtime. During the first week of a new pay period, Stefan worked 42.7 hours. In the second week of the pay period, he worked 44.6 hours. What was Stefan's total gross pay for these two weeks?

10. A part of the payroll record of the N & Y Plastic Molding Company is shown below. Overtime is paid when more than 8 hours are worked in a day. Time-and-a-half is paid for overtime. Figure these items for each employee and record them in the payroll record below: (a) total regular-time hours, (b) total overtime hours, (c) total earnings.

PAYROLL RECORD

For Week Ending: December 14, 20--

No.	Name	Time Record M	T	W	T	F	Pay Rate	Total Hours Regular	Overtime	Total Earnings
1	Dominic Fosse	7.5	8.0	8.7	9.3	5.0	$11.24			
2	Violet Hess	8.0	8.0	10.2	10.4	8.0	$10.68			
3	Hazel McGhee	8.0	7.0	9.2	8.4	8.0	$13.35			
4	Chuck Walden	8.1	8.0	9.4	9.1	8.0	$10.94			

                                    Chapter 1 Workbook

Lesson 1.4 *Commission*

Exercises

1. A salesperson who works on a straight commission basis sold 6 home air-conditioning systems at $2,320 each. The commission rate was 12%. What was the amount of commission?

2. Ingrid Sering sells two types of garden fountains on a straight commission basis. On one fountain that sells for $869, she gets a commission of $174. On the other fountain that sells for $1,260, she gets $252. During a 3-month selling season, Ingrid sold 19 of the lower-priced fountains and 23 of the higher-priced fountains. What were her total commissions for three months?

3. Isadore Vogt has a new sales job that pays a straight commission of 4% on all sales. The average weekly sales for his territory are $20,400. At this sales rate, how much could Isadore earn in one year of work, rounded to the nearest thousand?

4. Pauletta Detweiler is paid a salary of $325 a week plus $2\frac{3}{4}$% commission on weekly sales over $6,500. Her sales last week totaled $17,400. What were her total earnings for the week?

5. A store pays its salespeople on a salary plus commission basis. The store pays a 3.2% commission on sales over a weekly quota. The sales of four employees for last week are shown below. Find for each person the amount of commission and total earnings for the week.

	Salesperson	Sales	Quota	Commission	Salary	Total Earnings
a.	Homer Pedri	$12,980	$4,200		$310	
b.	Beth Adams	$11,600	$4,800		$350	
c.	Andrea Berger	$16,040	$4,500		$355	
d.	Keith Ryan	$10,800	$5,100		$370	

6. Wesley Bowman sells children's toy storage bins at craft shows. His commission is based on the number of bins sold in a month. He earns $45 each for the first 20 bins, $60 for the next 20 bins, and $75 for each bin over 40 bins. Wesley sold 28 sets in October and 56 in November. What was his total commission for the two months?

Lesson 1.4 *Commission*

7. MSA Products, Inc. pays it salespersons 6% commission on all sales and 3.5% more commission on all monthly sales over $40,000. In August, Giselle Campagna sold $56,000 worth of goods for MSA. What was her commission for August?

8. Nick Billups is paid a salary of $900 a month, a 2% commission on all sales, and 1.8% more on monthly sales over $17,500. In June, his sales were $48,500 and in July, $50,200. **a.** Find his total salary and commission for June. **b.** Find his total salary and commission for July.

9. Ann Wills is offered a sales job with two firms. Boden Tools offers her a salary of $800 a month, a commission of 3% on total monthly sales, and 3% more on monthly sales over $75,000. Sentor, Inc. offers her a commission of 2.5% on the first $45,000 of monthly sales, 4.5% on the next $20,000 of monthly sales, and 7% on all monthly sales over $65,000. If Ann could average $87,000 in sales a month at either job, at which job could she earn more per month, and how much more?

10. Find the amount of commission and the rate of commission, to the nearest tenth of a percent, paid on sales for each person.

	Name	Total Monthly Income	Salary	Sales	Amount of Commission	Rate of Commission
a.	Hewitt Van Lowe	$4,100	$800	$91,600		
b.	Bernyce Alger	$3,150	$1,270	$40,000		
c.	Moira Wade	$2,800	$700	$29,200		
d.	Burwell Crane	$5,600	$550	$194,230		

11. Myrtle Gould's total sales last month were $180,700, and her commission was $5,040. She earns a commission only on monthly sales over $50,000. Find her rate of commission to the nearest tenth percent.

Lesson 1.5 *Other Wage Plans*

Exercises

1. Custom Castings, Inc. pays its employees on a piece-rate basis of $1.28 for each acceptable piece produced. What gross pay was earned by an employee whose production of 483 pieces included 9 pieces that did not pass inspection?

2. Vernon Grimes produced these pieces during a week: Monday, 112; Tuesday, 107; Wednesday, 121; Thursday, 115; Friday, 97. If his employer pays $0.875 per piece produced, what would be Vernon's gross pay for the week?

3. The per diem employees listed below worked the number of days indicated in July. Find the gross pay earned by each employee.

	Employee	Occupation	Per Diem Rate	No. of Days Worked in July	Gross Pay
a.	Lorna Briggs	Accountant	$149.60	16	
b.	Edward Fielder	Lab Technician	$121.35	22	
c.	Orell Kantel	Laborer	$66.50	25	
d.	Shannon O'Hara	Tile Installer	$104.00	19	

4. Luther Bouchard delivers pizzas at his weekend job. On Saturday he delivered 40 pizzas to 26 homes. The average tip he received was $2.50 per stop. Luther was also paid $4 an hour for the 8 hours he worked on Saturday. Find his gross pay for Saturday.

5. Zeline Vanderbilt is a waitress in an upscale restaurant. On Friday she waited on 12 groups of customers who spent an average of $186 per group. Her tips averaged 18% of the total amount spent by all groups of customers that day. What were Zeline's tip income earnings that day?

Term Puzzler

Directions   Some of the terms listed below are in the puzzle. Circle each term when you find it. It may be written downward, upward, sideways, or diagonally. There are 19 terms in the puzzle. How many can you find?

- average
- commission
- double-time pay
- employee
- employer
- graduated commission
- gratuity
- gross pay
- gross wages
- hourly rate
- magnetic stripe card
- mean
- overtime
- per diem
- piece rate
- quota
- salaried employees
- salary
- simple average
- straight commission
- time-and-a-half-pay
- time card
- time sheet
- tip

N	P	G	R	O	S	S	W	A	G	E	S	M	E	I	D	R	E	P
V	D	Q	Z	R	E	K	C	R	K	M	F	L	G	D	X	V	S	I
H	O	U	R	L	Y	R	A	T	E	B	E	M	P	L	O	Y	E	E
M	U	O	V	E	R	T	I	M	E	S	H	E	E	T	G	L	M	C
O	B	T	G	O	U	G	R	O	S	S	P	A	Y	C	Z	P	B	E
V	L	A	F	I	A	E	J	L	W	S	G	N	D	E	L	F	E	R
T	E	P	T	K	J	B	G	F	Z	F	V	K	O	O	H	N	S	A
R	T	Y	Y	R	E	E	K	P	Y	P	F	O	Y	X	O	X	P	T
L	I	L	F	M	U	O	I	P	E	O	C	E	P	N	I	P	I	E
B	M	A	G	N	E	T	I	C	S	T	R	I	P	E	C	A	R	D
Y	E	F	C	O	M	M	I	S	S	I	O	N	B	K	U	C	H	K
T	P	S	G	G	M	A	B	M	A	V	E	R	A	G	E	X	H	G
S	A	A	V	K	D	N	K	S	E	L	F	D	F	R	O	R	B	W
D	Y	W	G	L	G	D	S	R	B	C	A	W	K	S	Q	C	Y	U
H	T	O	M	B	B	B	H	J	K	I	A	R	K	H	C	D	W	M
S	R	Y	D	L	C	P	D	X	L	I	T	R	Y	Y	T	G	J	C
S	O	J	Q	S	W	N	U	L	I	O	E	L	D	I	R	K	Y	G

　Name ____ Date ___________

Integrated Project 1

Directions Read through the entire project before you begin doing any work.

Introduction The Pro-Med Company builds custom-made equipment for research labs. Pro-Med's owner employs 11 workers to operate the company. Four employees build equipment to exact customer specifications. These employees are paid on a piece-rate basis. They work as a group and their pay is based on the total number of units built by the group in a week. They are paid a different rate per piece because their skills differ. Another three employees who are paid on an hourly basis test the custom-made equipment, repair equipment for customers, keep track of supplies, update production records, and ship equipment to customers.

Pro-Med's manager and an administrative assistant are paid a salary. The company also employs a sales representative who is paid a salary and commission. A temporary help agency provides an accountant for one and one-half days per week on a per diem basis.

The Pay Codes chart shown below lists pay codes and rates. The workers who are paid by hours worked or units produced receive pay that corresponds to their pay code. For example, a worker with a "C" pay code earns $17.90 an hour.

PRO-MED COMPANY, PAY CODES			
Hourly Rate Employees		Piece Rate Employees	
Pay Code	Hourly Rate	Pay Code	Piece Rate
A	$16.30	XA	$6.20
B	$17.15	XB	$8.50
C	$17.90	XC	$10.80
D	$18.75	XD	$12.90
E	$19.50	XE	$14.20

A Daily Hours Worked chart shows the hours worked for one week by each hourly rate employee. A Daily Unit Production chart shows the number of units produced each day by the work group. Notice that the group builds different types of products during the week.

Step One

1. Complete the Daily Hours Worked chart by finding the regular-time and overtime hours worked during the week by each employee. Overtime is based on a 40-hour week.

2. Complete the Daily Unit Production chart by finding the total number of units produced for the week. Do this by adding the number of units produced each day and for each product type. Write the daily sums on the "Totals" line and the product sums in the "Total Units Produced" column. Then take a corner total to find the total weekly production of the group.

Integrated Project 1, continued

<table>
<tr><td colspan="8">DAILY HOURS WORKED
Week Ending, August 20, 20--</td></tr>
<tr><td rowspan="2">Employee</td><td colspan="5">Hours Worked</td><td colspan="2">Total Hours Worked</td></tr>
<tr><td>M</td><td>TU</td><td>W</td><td>TH</td><td>F</td><td>Regular</td><td>Overtime</td></tr>
<tr><td>Branton, Miles</td><td>8.0</td><td>9.1</td><td>8.0</td><td>8.0</td><td>8.5</td><td></td><td></td></tr>
<tr><td>Hutton, Eunice</td><td>8.0</td><td>9.0</td><td>9.5</td><td>8.0</td><td>9.0</td><td></td><td></td></tr>
<tr><td>Powers, Alden</td><td>8.0</td><td>9.0</td><td>7.5</td><td>8.0</td><td>7.1</td><td></td><td></td></tr>
</table>

<table>
<tr><td colspan="7">DAILY UNIT PRODUCTION
Week Ending, August 20, 20--</td></tr>
<tr><td rowspan="2">Product Type</td><td colspan="5">Units Produced</td><td>Total Units Produced</td></tr>
<tr><td>M</td><td>TU</td><td>W</td><td>TH</td><td>F</td></tr>
<tr><td>T-12</td><td>8</td><td>11</td><td>0</td><td>8</td><td>2</td><td></td></tr>
<tr><td>T-13</td><td>0</td><td>6</td><td>15</td><td>0</td><td>16</td><td></td></tr>
<tr><td>T-24</td><td>9</td><td>0</td><td>1</td><td>13</td><td>0</td><td></td></tr>
<tr><td>Totals</td><td></td><td></td><td></td><td></td><td></td><td></td></tr>
</table>

Step Two

Complete the Payroll Sheet – Hourly & Piece-Rate Employees. Enter the pay rate for each employee. For hourly employees, enter the regular and overtime hours worked from the Daily Hours Worked chart. Then enter the total weekly production amount from the Daily Unit Production chart for piece-rate employees. Calculate the regular, overtime, and gross pay for hourly-rate employees and the gross pay for piece rate-employees. The overtime pay rate for hourly employees is 1.5 times the regular rate. Enter all data in the appropriate spaces on the Payroll Sheet. No data is to be entered in the shaded areas.

<table>
<tr><td colspan="9">PAYROLL SHEET — HOURLY and PIECE-RATE EMPLOYEES</td></tr>
<tr><td rowspan="2">Employee</td><td rowspan="2">Pay Code</td><td rowspan="2">Pay Rate</td><td rowspan="2">Total Weekly Production</td><td colspan="2">Hours Worked</td><td colspan="2">Pay</td><td rowspan="2">Gross Pay</td></tr>
<tr><td>Regular</td><td>Overtime</td><td>Regular</td><td>Overtime</td></tr>
<tr><td>Branton, Miles</td><td>B</td><td></td><td></td><td></td><td></td><td></td><td></td><td></td></tr>
<tr><td>Hutton, Eunice</td><td>D</td><td></td><td></td><td></td><td></td><td></td><td></td><td></td></tr>
<tr><td>Powers, Alden</td><td>A</td><td></td><td></td><td></td><td></td><td></td><td></td><td></td></tr>
<tr><td>Beresh, Sol</td><td>XA</td><td></td><td></td><td></td><td></td><td></td><td></td><td></td></tr>
<tr><td>Koss, Justine</td><td>XB</td><td></td><td></td><td></td><td></td><td></td><td></td><td></td></tr>
<tr><td>Pelletier, Vera</td><td>XE</td><td></td><td></td><td></td><td></td><td></td><td></td><td></td></tr>
<tr><td>Yang, Tas-fan</td><td>XC</td><td></td><td></td><td></td><td></td><td></td><td></td><td></td></tr>
</table>

Integrated Project 1, continued

Step Three

Answer the questions that follow about Pro-Med's weekly payroll.

3. What total amount of gross pay was paid for the week ending August 20 to hourly and piece-rate employees?

4. **a.** For the week ending August 20, what total amount of gross pay was paid to piece-rate employees?
   b. What average amount of piece-rate employees' total gross pay was spent to build each unit produced during the week of August 20, to the nearest cent?

5. The manager, Audrey Naumoff, is paid an annual salary of $74,000 a year. What is her monthly gross pay, rounded to the nearest dollar?

6. The annual salary of the administrative assistant, Edwin Brisbois, is $28,400. What weekly gross pay is Edwin paid, to the nearest cent?

7. Lorenzo Jordan, Pro-Med's salesperson, is paid a salary of $300 a week and a commission of 5% of average weekly sales. **a.** What is Lorenzo's gross pay for a week if sales average $30,000 weekly? **b.** At this weekly sales rate, how much would Lorenzo earn in a year?

8. The temporary help agency charges $185 per day for the per diem accountant. **a.** What amount was paid to the agency for the accountant's work for the week ending August 20? **b.** If the per diem rate and the days worked per week remain the same for an entire year, how much will Pro-Med spend for accountant services in one year?

     Chapter 1 *Workbook*

Lesson 2.1 *Deductions from Gross Pay*

Exercises

1. The form below shows the total wages, marital status, and withholding allowances for eight workers of Lemans, Inc. for the week of February 6. Use the withholding tax tables on page 41 in the textbook, of the textbook to find the withholding taxes. Use a social security tax rate of 6.2% and a Medicare tax rate of 1.45%. Write each amount in the proper column in the form.

Employee	Name	Married	Allowances	Total Wages	Income Tax	Social Security	Medicare
1	Alan, A.	Yes	3	602.27			
2	Berg, B.	No	1	410.98			
3	Cass, C.	No	1	389.87			
4	Dent, D.	Yes	4	625.55			
5	Evers, E.	Yes	2	501.87			
6	Ford, F.	Yes	5	599.57			
7	Gary, G.	No	2	497.55			
8	Houk, H.	No	1	421.76			

2. Complete the table below. Show for each worker (a) the social security tax (0.062), (b) Medicare tax (0.0145), (c) total deductions, and (d) net pay. Then find the total of each money column. Use the column totals to prove your work. The sum of the income tax, FICA tax, and other deductions column totals should equal the total deductions column total. The total wages minus the total deductions should equal the total net pay.

Emp No.	Name	Married	Allowances	Gross Wages	Income Tax	Social Security	Medicare	Other	Total Deduct.	Net Pay
					Deductions					
1	True, M.	Yes	5	535.88	8.00			85.12		
2	Ule, B.	No	2	545.71	49.00			75.34		
3	Vine, C.	Yes	2	502.77	23.00			75.34		
4	Wells, T.	No	1	375.99	33.00			58.89		
5	Yale, R.	No	1	456.76	45.00			55.25		
	Totals									

Bainbridge Company
Payroll Sheet for January 15, 20–

Lesson 2.1 *Deductions from Gross Pay*

3. Vera Nuños is single and claims one allowance. She works a 40-hour week at $12.75 an hour with time and a half for overtime. Last week she worked 42 hours. From her earnings, her employer deducted FICA tax at a rate of 7.65% and income tax using the withholding tax tables in Lesson 2.1. Her employer also deducted $64.50 for health insurance and $24.88 for union dues. Complete Vera's payroll form below.

Regular-time earnings	$ _____________
Overtime earnings	$ _____________
Total earnings	$ _____________
Deductions	
Income tax	$ _____________
FICA tax	$ _____________
Health insurance	$ _____________
Union dues	$ _____________
Total deductions	$ _____________
Net earnings	$ _____________

4. Calvin Peters earns $10.68 an hour for a $37\frac{1}{2}$-hour week. He is paid time and a half for time past $37\frac{1}{2}$ hours in a week. His employer deducts FICA tax at a rate of 7.65% and income tax of $60. His employer also deducts $65.37 per week for a health insurance plan that Calvin carries. Last week Calvin worked 44 hours. Complete his payroll form below.

Regular-time earnings	$ _____________
Overtime earnings	$ _____________
Total earnings	$ _____________
Deductions	
Income tax	$ _____________
FICA tax	$ _____________
Health insurance	$ _____________
Total deductions	$ _____________
Net earnings	$ _____________

Lesson 2.2 *Benefits and Job Expenses*

Exercises

1. Louise Vjotza is paid $11.75 an hour for a 40-hour week. Her employer also provides these fringe benefits: yearly pension contributions, $1,955.20; health and accident insurance per year, $1,267; free parking, $1,200 per year; free tuition for evening classes, $1,500 per year. **a.** What is Louise's annual wage? **b.** What are her total yearly fringe benefits? **c.** What are her total yearly job benefits?

2. Bea Williams is paid $2,883 a month. She estimates her yearly fringe benefits to be: pension contributions, $2,085; insurance, $645; free parking, $375; use of company car, $3,574. **a.** What is Bea's yearly pay? **b.** What are her total yearly fringe benefits? **c.** What are her total yearly job benefits?

3. Goro Unoji's job pays him $14.75 an hour for a 40-hour week. He estimates his fringe benefits to be 32% of his yearly wages. His yearly job expenses are estimated to be: union dues, $575; uniforms, $650; commuting costs, $1,294. **a.** What is Goro's total annual pay? **b.** What is the amount of his fringe benefits per year? **c.** What are his total yearly job benefits? **d.** What are his total yearly job expenses? **e.** What are his net yearly job benefits?

4. Julio Zapata has a job that pays $2,816 a month. He estimates that his fringe benefits are 28% of his annual wages. He also estimates that his yearly job expenses are special tools, $847; union dues, $970; commuting costs, $1,602; uniforms, $450. **a.** What is Julio's total annual pay? **b.** What is the amount of his annual fringe benefits? **c.** What are his total annual job benefits? **d.** What are his total annual job expenses? **e.** What are his net annual job benefits?

                                                      Chapter 2 *Workbook*

Lesson 2.2 *Benefits and Job Expenses*

5. Rita Falani has just graduated from school and is applying for two jobs. The first job pays $9.50 an hour for a 40-hour week and the second job pays $11.05 an hour for a 40-hour week. The fringe benefits are estimated to be 25% of the annual wage for the first job and 22% for the second. Yearly job expenses are estimated to be $1,480 for the first job and $1,796 for the second. **a.** Which job has the greater net yearly job benefits?   **b.** How much greater?

6. Consuela Lorenzo is comparing the four jobs below. Complete the form for her.

	Job 1	Job 2	Job 3	Job 4
Yearly Job Benefits				
Hourly wages for 40-hour week	$8.95	$8.50	$7.89	$9.50
Fringe benefits	19% of wages	19% of wages	25% of wages	18% of wages
Yearly Job Expenses				
Commuting costs	$256	$419	$899	$1,206
Uniforms	None	$560	None	$380
Union dues	$750	None	$1,200	None
Parking	$125	$430	$300	$620
Total Yearly				
Wages				
Fringe benefits				
Job benefits				
Job expenses				
Net job benefits				

Lesson 2.3 *Federal Income Taxes*

Exercises

1. Edna Kropp's gross income for a year included salary, $12,400; commission, $27,750; interest, $440. Her adjustments to income were payments to a retirement plan, $2,000, and a penalty for withdrawing savings early from a time-deposit account, $126.

   a. What was her gross income for the year?

   b. Find her adjusted gross income for the year.

2. Find the amounts that are missing from this summary of an income tax return:

a. Gross income	$42,685
b. Adjustments to income	3,670
c. Adjusted gross income	$_______
d. Deductions	8,978
e. Adjusted gross income less Deductions	$_______
f. Exemptions (4 × $3,100)	12,400
g. Taxable income	$_______

3. Vince Bottolito's adjusted gross income on his federal tax return was $53,748. He claimed the standard deduction of $4,850, and one exemption at $3,100. What was Vince's taxable income?

4. The Valek's gross income last year was $64,890. They had adjustments to income totaling $3,829. Their deductions totaled $12,502, and they had four exemptions at $3,100 each. Find their taxable income.

5. Ester Valdes earned $19,450 from wages, $4,000 from tips, and $1,467 in interest last year. She had adjustments to income of $2,157. She claimed the standard deduction of $4,850 and a personal exemption for herself of $3,100.

   a. What was Ester's gross income?

   b. What was her taxable income?

Lesson 2.3 *Federal Income Taxes*

6. Find the tax for each exercise. Use the tax table on page 55 in the textbook to do these exercises.

	Taxable Income	Filing status	Tax
a.	$13,585	Single	
b.	$13,800	Married filing jointly	
c.	$13,978	Head of household	
d.	$23,049	Married filing separately	
e.	$23,200	Married filing jointly	

7. Nicki Wilson is single and has a taxable income of $23,780. Find her tax.

8. Tim O'Hara's taxable income last year was $23,931.

   a. If Tim is single, what was his tax last year?

   b. If Tim is married and filing separately, what was his tax last year?

9. Mary Beth Sinclair's employer withheld $1,851 for taxes last year from her wages. On her tax return, Mary's taxable income was $13,587 and her filing status was "married filing separately."

   a. Should Mary pay additional tax or receive a refund?

   b. What is the amount of the payment or refund?

10. The Kokorapolus's are married and are filing a joint tax return. Their gross income is $35,836. They are claiming $1,000 in adjustments to income. They are also claiming $8,906 in itemized deductions and four exemptions of $3,100 each. They have already paid a total of $2,245 in withholding taxes.

    a. What was their actual tax?

    b. They are entitled to a refund of what amount?

       Chapter 2 *Workbook*

Lesson 2.3 *Federal Income Taxes*

Use the tax table on page 55 in the textbook to solve these exercises. Assume that every person was listed on his or her parents' return as a dependent and will claim the standard deduction rather than itemize.

11. Vera worked as a landscape gardener for 20 weeks last year to help earn money for school. She worked 15 hours each week at $8.25 an hour. Her employer deducted $11 each week for federal withholding taxes. Vera also earned $308.62 in interest on her savings account. Complete the form below:

Wages	
Interest	
Adjusted Gross Income	
Less Deductions	
Taxable Income	
Tax from table in Lesson 2.3	
Amount of Tax Withheld	
Refund Due	

12. Victor earned $3,452 in wages last year as a part-time stock clerk and $216 in interest. His employer withheld $325 in federal income taxes from his wages.

    a. What was Victor's taxable income?

    b. How much will Victor receive as a refund from federal taxes?

13. Anna Mareno earned $5,119 working part-time last year. The total federal withholding taxes she paid were $480. Anna also earned $128 in interest. How much should she receive as a tax refund from the federal government?

Lesson 2.4 *State and City Income Taxes*

Exercises

1. Susan Wong's taxable income last year was $52,915. The income tax rate in her state is 2% of taxable income. What was Susan's tax last year?

2. Ira Rothman lives in Tennyson. Residents of Tennyson pay a city income tax of 2% of their taxable income per year. Find Rothman's tax on his taxable income of $34,800.

3. Use these state income tax rates to find the income tax for four taxpayers.

Tax Rates	Taxpayer	Taxable Income	Income Tax
1% of the first $5,000 of taxable income	a. Rim Beale	$ 6,000	
2% of the next $15,000 of taxable income	b. Vi Wilder	$24,800	
3% of the next $20,000 of taxable income	c. Juan Pujols	$46,900	
4% of all taxable income over $40,000	d. Bev Olds	$98,310	

These are the state and city income tax rates in Thomasville.

State Tax Rates		**City Tax Rates**	
Rate	Taxable Income	Rate	Taxable Income
2%	First $5,000	1%	First $ 15,000
3%	Next $10,000	2%	All over $15,000
4%	All over $15,000		

4. Rob Torre lives in Thomasville and has a taxable income of $31,500 for a year. **a.** What was Rob's state income tax for the year? **b.** What was Rob's city income tax? **c.** What was Rob's total state and city income tax?

Lesson 2.5   *Cash Receipts and Payments Records*

Exercises

1. The cash receipts record of Anna Estaban is on the right. Anna is an office worker at a brokerage firm and has a part-time job on weekends. Add the amounts in the "Amount" column and write the total on the "Total" line.

Anna Esteban
Cash Receipts Record

Date	Explanation	Amount
July 1	Interest on savings	15.98
2	Birthday gift	50.00
6	Full-time pay	475.00
8	Part-time pay	96.00
13	Full-time pay	475.00
15	Part-time pay	64.00
20	Full-time pay	475.00
22	Part-time pay	96.00
27	Full-time pay	475.00
29	Part-time pay	96.00
30	Purchase rebate check	25.00
	Total	

2. The Future Business Leaders of America at Mt. Vernon High School sold soda at basketball games. For five games, their receipts were $147.16, $132.66, $195.22, $98.88, and $128.72. What were the total receipts for the games?

3. The pony ride at a town homecoming fair had the following receipts for the three-day event: $143.75, $166.25, and $132.50. What were the ride's total receipts for the fair?

4. A botanical garden's cashier received the following amounts of money for 10 weeks in the summer:

$1,361.75	$2,247.75
1,467.25	1,870.75
2,128.75	1,506.25
1,613.25	1,935.75
1,957.50	2,157.75

What was the total amount received by the cashier?

        Chapter 2 *Workbook*

Lesson 2.5   *Cash Receipts and Payments Records*

5. Complete the cash payments record with special columns below. Check your work by adding horizontally the totals of each of the Type of Payment columns.

Week	Type of Payment					Total Payment
	Rent	Food	Clothing	Other	Savings	
Oct. 1-7	875.00	156.22	201.89	25.00	100.00	
8-14		135.88		15.98		
15-21		187.96		123.73	100.00	
22-28		184.55	156.89	57.61		
29-31		92.45		88.50		
Totals						

6. Complete the cash payments record with special columns below. Check your work by adding horizontally the totals of each of the Type of Payment columns.

Week	Type of Payment						Total Payment
	Rent	Food	Auto	Personal Care	Other	Savings	
June 1-7	725.00	188.54	325.89	125.00	56.66	150.00	
8-14		105.20	35.22	26.78	27.98		
15-21		88.56	157.80	85.79	26.45	150.00	
22-28		195.76	37.49	25.68	126.79		
29-30		53.44	15.80	48.79	88.76		
Totals							

Lesson 2.6 *Budgets*

Exercises

1. Eve Soulard's monthly cash record summary is shown below. Add each expense row horizontally to find the total payments. Then add each column and write the total on the line labeled "Totals." Check your work by adding the totals of the six types of payments columns. The total of these columns should equal the total of the Payments column.

Month	Receipts	Payments	Type of Payments (Expenses)					
			Food	Clothing	Housing	Auto	Other	Savings
January	2,158.00		425.34	125.32	650.00	542.89	124.32	50.00
February	2,158.00		489.21	67.88	650.00	567.58	66.93	50.00
March	2,158.00		445.24	45.78	650.00	605.12	205.64	50.00
April	2,158.00		581.12	278.52	650.00	558.21	305.77	50.00
May	2,158.00		498.65	67.45	650.00	489.75	109.56	50.00
June	2,158.00		578.55	109.68	650.00	665.88	521.21	50.00
July	2,225.00		601.21	215.45	650.00	576.97	89.45	50.00
August	2,225.00		476.55	312.45	650.00	586.45	221.28	50.00
September	2,225.00		567.94	37.89	650.00	501.88	186.45	50.00
October	2,225.00		548.37	54.78	650.00	678.20	215.45	50.00
November	2,225.00		654.21	224.51	650.00	600.87	221.21	50.00
December	2,500.00		624.12	258.45	650.00	486.77	105.88	50.00
Totals								

2. Based on the totals of the cash summary above, what percent, to the nearest tenth, of the total payments for the year were Eve's:

   a. Food payment?

   b. Auto payment?

   c. Savings?

Lesson 2.6 *Budgets*

3. Oscar Laraunt's monthly take-home pay is $1,800. His expenses last month are shown below. In the blanks provided, write the fractional part of his take-home pay that he spent for each item.

    a. Food $600, or

    b. Auto $300, or

    c. Clothing $180, or

    d. Other $60, or

    e. Housing $540, or

    f. Savings $120, or

4. Rosa Miranda estimates that her total cash income for the year will be $30,000. She plans to spend her income as shown below. Write in the spaces provided the amounts allowed for each item.

    a. Food 26%, or

    b. Auto 21%, or

    c. Clothing 11%, or

    d. Other 10%, or

    e. Housing 30%, or

    f. Savings 5%, or

5. Ramon Lugo is given $600 a month for college living expenses. His budget for this month is shown below. Find what percent of his monthly income is budgeted for each item, to the nearest tenth percent.

    a. Clothing $45, or

    b. Housing $240, or

    c. Food $185, or

    d. Transportation $50, or

    e. Recreation $55, or

    f. Other $25, or

Lesson 2.6 *Budgets*

6. Sapersons, a sporting equipment chain, expects to gain extra sales of $650,000 on a sales promotion. It plans to spend these percents of the extra sales on the promotion: newspaper advertising, 4.5%; radio advertising, 2.7%; television advertising, 2.3%; other advertising, 0.5%. The firm plans to spend these amounts for each type of advertising:

    a. Newspaper

    b. Radio

    c. Television

    d. Other

7. Alice and Clark O'Malley have a monthly income of $4,200. They plan to spend their income as shown in the chart on the right. Find the amount they plan to spend this year for each item in the chart.

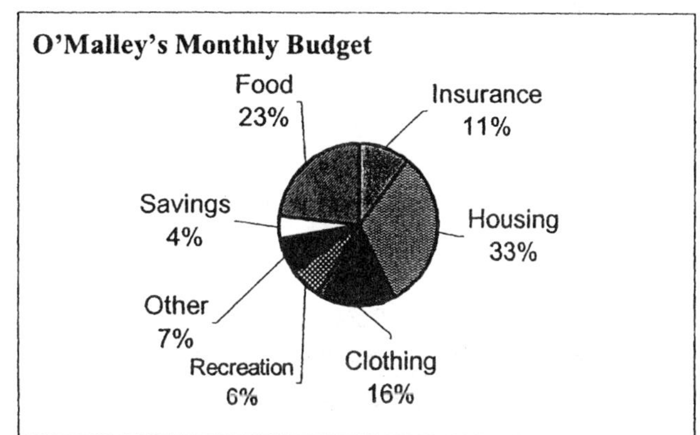

    a. Food

    b. Clothing

    c. Housing

    d. Insurance

    e. Recreation

    f. Other

    g. Savings

Name _________________________________ Date ___________

Term Puzzler

Complete the crossword puzzle below. Some answers are two words placed together without space between them.

Across

3. A tax rate that is fixed regardless of income
4. Adjusted gross income less deductions and exemptions
6. Hospital insurance for the disabled or retired
9. A form showing how much you owe in taxes
11. Gross pay less deductions
13. Money deducted from wages for income taxes
14. Benefits of value employees get in addition to wages
16. A type of addition used to check addition

Down

1. Actual tax deductions that are more than standard deduction
2. Income per person that is free from tax
3. Income that does not vary
5. Future spending plans
7. Expenses that may change each period
8. Addition across
10. Reduces the amount of withholding taxes
12. What you get back if you overpay taxes
15. Corner total used to check the accuracy of a table

Chapter 2 *Workbook*

Integrated Project 2

Directions Read through the entire project before you begin doing any work.

Introduction Twanya and Lewellyn Madison are married and have one son. Twanya works part-time and Lewellyn works full-time as salesclerks in the same department store.

Step One

The Madisons must complete their joint federal income tax return for last year's income. Their gross income last year was $44,150. They had adjustments to income for an approved retirement plan of $2,870. They also itemized their deductions and found a total of $8,380. They claimed three exemptions (one each for Twanya, Lewellyn, and their son) at $3,100 each.

    1. What is their taxable income?

    2. Using the table on page 55 in the textbook, what is the amount of their federal income tax?

    3. The Madisons' employer deducted $2,704 in federal withholding taxes during the year. Will the Madisons have to pay more taxes or will they receive a refund, and what is the amount?

Step Two

The Madisons also must complete a state income tax return and pay a tax on the amount of taxable income shown on their federal return.

    4. Using the table on page 61 in the textbook, what is the amount of their state income tax?

    5. The Madisons' employer deducted $706 in state withholding taxes during the year. Will they have to pay more state income taxes or will they receive a refund, and what is the amount?

Step Three

The Madisons' son, Dwayne, earned $2,130 last summer to help with the cost of his schooling. He also earned $84 in interest through his savings account. His employer deducted $256 in federal and $78 in state withholding taxes. Dwayne needs to complete state and federal income tax returns in order to get refunds of the taxes that were withheld from his wages.

    6. Using the table on page 55 of the textbook, find the amount of Dwayne's federal income tax. He claims the standard deduction, which is a minimum of $800 and a maximum of $4,850.

                                                         Chapter 2 *Workbook*

Integrated Project 2, continued

7. How much federal income tax refund should Dwayne expect?

8. Using the table on page 61 of the textbook, find the amount of Dwayne's state income tax.

9. How much state income tax refund should Dwayne expect?

Step Four

All the Madisons paid FICA taxes at 7.65% on their gross wages.

10. How much FICA taxes did the parents pay?

11. How much FICA taxes did Dwayne pay?

12. What total amount of state income, federal income, and FICA taxes did the parents pay?

13. What total amount of state income, federal income, and FICA taxes did Dwayne pay?

Step Five

The Madisons want to budget their income. They estimate that their net income this year will be $39,000. The percentages below show how they plan to spend the net income.

14. Find the dollar amount they plan to spend on each type of expense.

Expenses	Percent	Amount
Food	25%	
Clothing	10%	
Housing	28%	
Transportation	14%	
Other	17%	
Savings	6%	

Lesson 3.1 *Checking Accounts*

Exercises

1. Conrad and Maureen Clay have these items to deposit on October 24: (bills) \$36; (coins) \$12.50; (checks) \$768.14, \$25, \$2.40. No cash was received. Complete the Clay's deposit slip.

For deposit to the account of

CONRAD AND MAUREEN CLAY

Date _October 24,_ 20—

Riverside National Bank
St. Louis, MO

Subject to the terms and conditions of the
Bank's Collection Agreement

⑆:02810 0735⑈ 13 61502

Cash including coins		
Checks		
Check or Total From Other Side		
SUB TOTAL		
Less Cash Received		
TOTAL DEPOSIT	\$	

2. Celine Coulter has this deposit to make on January 8: (coins) 60 quarters, 150 pennies; (checks) \$582.13, \$76.21. She wants cash back of \$120. Complete Celine's deposit slip.

For deposit to the account of

CELINE COULTER

Date _January 8,_ 20—

Edgemont Bank and Trust Company
St. Louis, MO

Subject to the terms and conditions of the
Bank's Collection Agreement

⑆:02810 06219⑈ 15 98632

Cash including coins		
Checks		
Check or Total From Other Side		
SUB TOTAL		
Less Cash Received		
TOTAL DEPOSIT	\$	

3. Universal Sports' bank deposit includes these items: (bills) 10 hundreds, 18 fifties, 90 twenties, 40 tens; (checks) \$19.20, \$562.78, \$125.04. Universal wants cash back of 6 rolls of pennies (50 pennies to a roll), 8 rolls of nickels (40 nickels to a roll), 5 rolls of dimes (50 dimes to a roll), 4 rolls of quarters (40 quarters to a roll), and 100 one-dollar bills. Complete Universal's deposit slip.

For deposit to the account of

Universal Sports

Date _April 12,_ 20—

Edgemont Bank and Trust Company
St. Louis, MO

Subject to the terms and conditions of the
Bank's Collection Agreement

⑆:02810 06219⑈ 18 98714

Cash including coins		
Checks		
Check or Total From Other Side		
SUB TOTAL		
Less Cash Received		
TOTAL DEPOSIT	\$	

Lesson 3.1 *Checking Accounts*

4. Giselle Dostal's check register had a balance of $618.07 on February 16. She wrote these checks on February 18: 1182 to Edwin's Towing for $45; 1183 to Farwell Clothiers for $129.16. She deposited her pay of $515.35 on February 19. Record these items in Giselle's check register and take a running balance.

Check Register

Check No.	Date	Description of Transaction	Payment/Debit		Deposit/Credit		Balance	

5. The check register of DeWitt Hammond showed a balance of $496.42 on July 11. He deposited a payroll check of $318.91 on July 12. On July 13 these checks were written: 121 for $525 to Harwell Apartments; 122 for $98.08 to Newman Credit; and 123 for $75 to United Way. Record these transactions and take a running balance.

Check Register

Check No.	Date	Description of Transaction	Payment/Debit		Deposit/Credit		Balance	

6. Celia Stavros' check register showed a balance of $1,914.56 on April 12. On April 13, Check 516 for $282.87 was made payable to the U. S. Treasury. A net deposit of $678.42 was made on April 15. These checks were written on April 18: 517 to Foster Markets, $96.24; 518 to Glasko Auto, $314.48; 519 to Body Tone Health Club, $95. Record these transactions and take a running balance.

Check Register

Check No.	Date	Description of Transaction	Payment/Debit		Deposit/Credit		Balance	

Chapter 3 *Workbook*

Lesson 3.2 *Electronic Banking*

Exercises

1. On Sunday, Hattie St. Aubin used an ATM to deposit a check for $613.15 and to withdraw $125 in cash for shopping. If her starting bank balance was $211.76, what is her new balance after these transactions are processed?

2. Stephen Awrey used a debit card to pay for the following three purchases: groceries, $91.34; auto parts, $18.50; scanner, $196.18. If Stephen's bank balance was $432.78 at the start of the day, what is his new balance?

3. On Wednesday morning, Russell Hobart deposited a tax refund check for $127.56 in his bank's ATM and also withdrew $80 cash from the ATM. He then used his debit card to make these purchases: books, $38.24; set of dishes, $148.09; concert tickets, $76.50. If his starting bank balance was $891.58, what is his new balance?

4. Rosaria Shearer started the day with a bank balance of $1,011.86. She used an ATM to deposit a check for $136 and withdrew $140 in cash. She made these purchases with a debit card: kitchen table and chairs, $643.24; unfinished bookcase, $98.45; greeting cards, $12.50. What is the balance in Rosaria's bank account when the transactions are processed?

5. Gunther Flieghe had a bank balance of $782.23 on Monday. On Tuesday, he made debit purchases for $128.39, $29.32, and $78.92. On Wednesday, he used his bank's ATM to withdraw $100 cash. A direct deposit of Gunther's paycheck for $611.45 was made at noon on Friday. On Friday evening Gunther used his debit card to pay a restaurant bill of $32.43. What was Gunther's bank balance after these transactions were posted?

                                                    Chapter 3 *Workbook*

     Name ____ Date ___________

Lesson 3.3 *Online Banking*

Exercises

1. Oswald Prost's online accounts had these balances on Sunday, October 2: checking. $214.06; savings, $872.83. On Monday, October 3, Oswald made an ATM withdrawal of $60 from his checking account. He plans to make these online payments on Tuesday, October 4: rent, $460; telephone bill, $38.12; charge account bill, $316.81. How much money must Oswald transfer from savings to checking on Tuesday to make the EFT payments and leave a minimum of $120 in the checking account?

2. Rosalie Cambron had online accounts that showed a balance of $116.71 in checking and $982.56 in savings on Tuesday, January 12. A direct deposit of her weekly pay of $789.43 was made on Wednesday, January 13 to her checking account. On her way home from work Rosalie used an ATM to withdraw $40 from checking. She wants to make these online payments on Wednesday evening: car loan, $360.18; electric bill, $47.02; property taxes, $954.56. What amount must Rosalie transfer to her checking account from savings on Wednesday to make the payments and leave a minimum of $50 in checking?

3. The online bank accounts of Harvey Baird had these balances on Monday: checking, $82.18; savings, $521.64. Harvey expects to have these EFT transactions over the next five days: online payment of auto insurance of $484.90 on Wednesday; direct deposit of a $514.92 paycheck to checking on Friday; ATM withdrawal of $100 from checking on Saturday; online payment of $35.15 on Saturday for cable service. Harvey wants to maintain a minimum balance of $75 in checking at all times and will transfer money from savings to checking whenever necessary.

   a. On which day(s) must Harvey transfer money from savings to checking, and in what amount(s)?

   b. What will be the balance of his checking account on Saturday after all transactions are processed?

4. The balances in Jessica Tuttle's online accounts on Friday morning were checking, $76.14, and savings, $1,800.56. On Friday evening Jessica plans her EFT transactions through the weekend. The bills due on Friday that will be paid online include: home loan, $761; charge account, $112.87; water bill, $76.18. Jessica plans to make a $150 ATM withdrawal from checking on Saturday morning. **a.** What amount must Jessica transfer from savings to checking on Friday to cover these transactions so that she will have a minimum balance of $70 in her checking account on Saturday afternoon? **b.** What will be the balance of the savings account after the transfer is made?

Lesson 3.4 *Check Register Reconciliation*

Exercises

1. Olga Gleason's bank statement balance on March 31 was $2,371.40. On the same date, her check register balance was $1,732.39. The bank statement showed a service charge of $8.30 and interest earned of $1.12. The checkbook showed three outstanding checks: No. 988 for $173.19, No. 990 for $417.28, and No. 991 for $55.72. Reconcile Olga's bank statement and check register.

Reconciliation Form		
Follow these steps:		Outstanding Checks
Enter closing balance from statement		
Add any deposits outstanding	+	
Add lines 1 and 2		
Enter total of outstanding checks	–	
Subtract line 4 from 3. This amount should equal your check register balance.		Total $

Check Register

Check No.	Date	Description of Transaction	Payment/Debit	Deposit/Credit	Balance

2. Chikabumi Onodera's check register balance on September 30 was $466.23. On the same date, the bank statement showed a balance of $590.51. Included on the statement were three items not recorded in the check register: service charge of $5.40, interest earned of $0.68, and an ATM deposit for $129. Reconcile Chikabumi's check register.

Check Register

Check No.	Date	Description of Transaction	Payment/Debit	Deposit/Credit	Balance

Lesson 3.4 *Check Register Reconciliation*

3. Sheldon Jennings' check register balance on July 31 was $525.58. His bank statement balance on July 31 was $610.91. When he compared his check register with his bank statement, the statement showed a service charge of $12.75 and interest earned of $1.01. His check register showed three outstanding checks: No. 675 for $89.32, No. 676 for $21.18, and No. 679 for $200.57. Also, a deposit of $214 was made too late to appear on the statement. Reconcile Sheldon's bank statement and check register.

Reconciliation Form		
Follow these steps:		Outstanding Checks
Enter closing balance from statement		
Add any deposits outstanding	+	
Add lines 1 and 2		
Enter total of outstanding checks	–	
Subtract line 4 from 3. This amount should equal your check register balance.		Total

Check Register

Check No.	Date	Description of Transaction	Payment/Debit	Deposit/Credit	Balance

4. On December 31, Hertha Bauer's check register balance was $265.86 and her bank statement balance was $599.42. The total amount of deposits on the statement was $456.12 and the total amount of checks was $500.23. The statement also showed a service charge of $2.45, $17.75 charge for printed checks, and a deposit of $235.67 that had not been recorded in the check register. There was one outstanding check for $118.09. Reconcile her check register.

Check Register

Check No.	Date	Description of Transaction	Payment/Debit	Deposit/Credit	Balance

Lesson 3.5 *Other Reconciliation Problems*

Exercises

1. On July 31, Ilene Darin's bank statement showed a balance of $1,001.79. Her check register's balance was $718.29. While comparing the bank statement to the check register Ilene found a service charge of $13.65, that Check 367 for $76.09 had been recorded in the check register as $67.09, a deposit of $194.35 made on July 10 had not been recorded in the check register, and Check 371 for $47.36 had been recorded twice in the check register. An EFT loan payment for $159.10 also was not recorded in the check register. A deposit of $350 was recorded in the check register but was made too late to appear on the bank statement. Outstanding checks were 363 for $157.73 and 374 for $415.81. Reconcile Ilene's bank statement and check register.

Reconciliation Form			
Follow these steps:		Outstanding	
		Checks	
Enter closing balance from statement			
Add any deposits outstanding	+		
Add lines 1 and 2			
Enter total of outstanding checks	−		
Subtract line 4 from 3. This amount			
should equal your check register balance.		Total	

Check Register

Check No.	Date	Description of Transaction	Payment/Debit	Deposit/Credit	Balance

Lesson 3.5 *Other Reconciliation Problems*

2. On February 28, Woodrow Fraser's check register balance was $424.09 and his bank statement balance was $343.15. Comparing the register with the bank statement, he found a service charge for $13.50 and interest earned of $0.92 listed on the statement. He also found that he had failed to record Check 986 to Schiller Furniture for $135.65, an ATM withdrawal for $70, and an ATM-user fee of $1.50 in his check register. Also, Check 985 for $86.32 was recorded in the register as $86.23. Outstanding checks were 988 for $18.15 and 989 for $268.73. A deposit mailed on February 26 for $148 was not listed on the bank statement. Reconcile Woodrow's bank statement and check register.

Reconciliation Form		
Follow these steps:		Outstanding Checks
Enter closing balance from statement		
Add any deposits outstanding	+	
Add lines 1 and 2		
Enter total of outstanding checks	−	
Subtract line 4 from 3. This amount should equal your check register balance.		Total

Check Register

Check No.	Date	Description of Transaction	Payment/Debit		Deposit/Credit		Balance	

Lesson 3.6 *Savings Accounts*

Exercises

1. Find the interest for one interest period for each exercise. Round your answers to the nearest cent. Write your answers in the amount of interest column.

	Account Balance	Annual Rate of Interest	Interest Period	Amount of Interest
a.	$438	3.00%	quarter	
b.	$306	5.00%	semiannual	
c.	$973	4.30%	quarter	
d.	$892	$5\frac{1}{2}\%$	quarter	
e.	$471	$3\frac{1}{4}\%$	semiannual	
f.	$849	6.00%	quarter	
g.	$529	7.00%	semiannual	
h.	$726	4.35%	quarter	
i.	$685	5.10%	quarter	
j.	$729	6.80%	semiannual	

2. A savings account deposit of $8,500 is made on April 1 and kept on deposit for 3 months. The account earns 5.4% annual interest, compounded quarterly. What amount of interest is earned on the deposit for three months?

3. What interest could be earned by a deposit of $1,500 for 6 months at a bank that pays a $4\frac{1}{8}\%$ annual interest rate, compounded semiannually?

4. These banks pay annual interest on savings accounts as follows: First Valley Bank, 4.1%; Serco Bank, 3.85%. What is the difference in the interest paid by these banks if $20,000 is kept on deposit for one year?

5. The amount of interest you could earn in six months on a $12,000 deposit in the Fiftieth State Bank that pays quarterly interest is $180.68. Could you earn more interest for the half-year by depositing $12,000 in an account that pays a 3.1% annual interest rate? How much more?

Lesson 3.6 *Savings Accounts*

Find the interest paid and the balance for each date listed in each savings account. Write your answers in the table. Interest is compounded quarterly on January 1, April 1, July 1, and October 1. Semiannual interest is paid on January 1 and July 1.

6.

Annual interest rate: 4%		
Interest paid: quarterly		
Date	**Interest**	**Balance**
Oct. 1		$900.00
Jan. 1		
Apr.1		
July 1		
Oct. 1		

7.

Annual interest rate: 5.3%		
Interest paid: semiannually		
Date	**Interest**	**Balance**
Jan. 1		$1,250.00
July 1		
Jan. 1		
July 1		
Jan. 1		

8.

Annual interest rate: $3\frac{1}{2}$ %		
Interest paid: quarterly		
Date	**Interest**	**Balance**
Apr. 1		$790.00
July 1		
Oct. 1		
Jan. 1		
Apr. 1		

9.

Annual interest rate: $4\frac{3}{4}$ %		
Interest paid: semiannually		
Date	**Interest**	**Balance**
July 1		$2,600.00
Jan. 1		
July 1		
Jan. 1		

For each exercise use the compound interest table in Chapter 3 of the textbook to find the compound amount and compound interest.

	Beginning Principal	Annual Rate	Time	Compounding Period	Compound Amount	Compound Interest
10.	$3,000	1%	5 years	annual		
11.	$2,200	4%	9 years	annual		
12.	$900	5%	180 days	daily		
13.	$2,500	$2\frac{1}{2}$ %	90 days	daily		
14.	$500	10%	3 years	semiannual		
15.	$1,400	3%	4 years	semiannual		
16.	$3,600	8%	3 years	quarter		
17.	$870	5%	2 years	quarter		
18.	$1,350	2%	7 years	annual		

Lesson 3.7 *Money Market and CD Accounts*

Exercises

1. Marcella Burgess deposited $15,000 for two months in a money-market account that pays simple interest. For the first month, Marcella earned 3.87% annual interest. She earned 3.47% annual interest for the second month. Interest is not compounded. What total interest did Marcella earn in two months?

2. Edwin Pritchard deposited $7,500 in a 3-year, time-deposit account that pays simple interest at a 5.9% annual rate. What total amount of interest will Edwin's deposit earn in three years?

3. Gladys McPherson deposited $42,000 for two months in a compound-interest money-market account that paid 4.18% annual interest the first month and 4.08% the second month. She could have deposited her money for two months in another bank's money market account that guaranteed a simple interest rate of 4.13% for both months. In which plan could Gladys have earned the most interest?

Find the amount of the penalty based on the amount withdrawn. Then find the net interest.

	Amount of Deposit	Interest Earned to Date	Amount Withdrawn Early	Penalty		Net Interest
				Charge	Amount	
4.	$24,000	$900.00	$6,000	1 month's interest at 5%		
5.	$11,000	$577.50	$3,500	6 month's interest at 7%		
6.	$5,000	$1,600.00	$5,000	12 month's interest at 8%		
7.	$25,000	$812.50	$4,000	3 month's interest at 6.5%		
8.	$8,000	$70.00	$8,000	2 month's interest at 5.25%		

Lesson 3.7 *Money Market and CD Accounts*

For each deposit in Exercises 9 -13, find the amount of interest that could be earned in a passbook account and a certificate of deposit account. Then find the difference between the amount of passbook interest and certificate of deposit interest.

	Amount of Deposit	Time Money Is on Deposit	Passbook Interest Rate	Amount	Certificate Interest Rate	Amount	Difference Between Passbook Interest and Certificate Interest
9.	$4,000	3 months	3.50%		7.00%		
10.	$18,000	6 months	2.40%		4.75%		
11.	$9,500	12 months	4.12%		6.50%		
12.	$36,000	9 months	2.25%		5.10%		
13.	$21,000	4 months	3.75%		6.30%		

For Exercises 14-16 use the compound interest table on page 113 in Lesson 3.6 to find the annual interest earned. Then calculate the effective rate of interest.

14. Arnold Landis made a deposit of $720 to open a savings account that pays interest at an annual rate of 5%, compounded quarterly. **a.** If he keeps his original deposit in the savings account and is paid interest for four quarters, how much interest will he earn in the first year? **b.** What is the effective rate of interest that his deposit will earn, to the nearest hundredth percent?

15. Rebecca Ellis' bank pays 8% annual interest on savings accounts, compounded quarterly. On April 1, she made a deposit of $1,500 to her savings account, which had a balance of $400. **a.** She makes no other deposits or withdrawals to the account for one year. On the following April 1 what will her account balance be? **b.** What interest amount will she have earned? **c.** The interest named in part b represents what effective rate of interest, to the nearest hundredth percent?

16. A bank offers a savings account that pays 6% annual interest, compounded quarterly. **a.** A deposit of $7,850 held in the bank for one year would earn how much interest? **b.** This amount is equivalent to what effective rate of interest, to the nearest hundredth percent?

Term Puzzler

Directions Each group of scrambled letters can be sorted to spell a word or phrase. Unscramble the letters to form a word or phrase. Then sort the letters in boxes to form a key word.

a. Sort the scrambled letters below.

1. pcumoodn notuam

2. etnitser

3. ibetd radc

4. kchce gsietrre

5. tedcir potsied

6. akbn ttatnemse

7. colairencinoit

8. rumtyati edta

9. eiolnn kabgnin

10. tidspoe lspi

11. lacebna

b. The key word is ___________________________.

Name ____ Date ____________

Integrated Project 3

Directions Read through the entire project before you begin doing any work.

Background Tamyra Gregory moved to a new city recently and opened a checking account and savings account at the Ridgeview National Bank on May 1. The original deposits were $1,800 to checking and $9,800 to savings. Tamyra's checking account is "free" as long as she keeps $2,000 on deposit in a savings account with Ridgeview National. She is paid interest on the average daily balance in her checking account. Tamyra was given a debit card that she may use for ATM transactions and to make debit purchases.

Ridgeview National sends statements of account to its customers within one week after the end of the month. The statement prepared June 6 covers transactions in her checking and savings accounts for the previous month. Tamyra's May bank statement which she received on June 7 covers the period of May 1 to May 31.

Step One

Compare the Checking Account Summary portion of the bank statement with the check register. Place a check mark next to the items in the bank statement and in the √ column of the check register when items on both forms agree. On the bank statement only, place an "X" next to the items that are not found in the check register. Items in the check register that do not have a check mark in the √ column are *not* to be marked in any way until you are directed to do so in Step Two. You are to reconcile differences between the bank statement and check register by using the bank reconciliation form provided and by recording the necessary entries in the check register.

Reconciliation Form		
Follow these steps:		Outstanding Checks
Enter closing balance from statement		
Add any deposits outstanding	+	
Add items 1 and 2		
Enter total of outstanding checks	–	
Subtract line 4 from 3. This amount should equal your check register balance.		Total

Integrated Project 3, continued

Statement of Account

Statement Prepared June 6, 20—
Checking Account Summary:

Ridgeview National Bank	05/01	Balance Brought Forward	$ 0.00
		+ Deposits	5474.00
Tamyra Gregory		– Checks	2553.91
555 Main Street		– Other Charges	753.26
Ridgeview, IL	05/31	Closing Balance	2166.83

Checks

Check	Date	Amount	Check	Date	Amount	Check	Date	Amount
001	05/06	590.00	004	05/13	460.21	008	05/31	142.20
002	05/10	86.05	005	05/21	416.28			
003	05/11	170.00	007	05/31	689.17			

Total Checks 2,553.91

Deposits

Date	Explanation	Amount
05/01	Opening Deposit	1800.00
05/06	Deposit	790.46
05/12	Deposit	511.08
05/13	Deposit	790.46
05/20	Deposit	790.46
05/27	Direct Deposit	790.46
05/31	Interest Earned	1.08

Total Deposits 5,474.00

Other Charges

Date	Explanation	Amount
05/06	DEBIT, Leah's Fashions	187.27
05/11	ATM Withdrawal, Sawmill County Bank	200.00
05/11	ATM User Fee, Sawmill County Bank	1.25
05/27	ATM Withdrawal, Ridgeview Bank	180.00
05/28	DEBIT, Lauder Department Store	65.84
05/31	DEBIT, Holder Lake Sports, Inc.	118.90

Total Other Charges 753.26

Savings Account Summary

Date	Explanation	Amount
05/01	Opening Deposit	9500.00
05/31	Interest (1.5% Annual Rate)	11.88
05/31	Balance	9511.88

Name ____ Date _____________

Integrated Project 3, *continued*

Check Register

Check No.	Date	Description	Payment/Debit		Deposit/Credit		√	Balance	
	05/01	Opening Deposit						1,800	00
001	05/04	Village Rentals	590	00				1,210	00
002	05/06	Ameriwide Cable	86	50				1,123	50
	05/06	Deposit, Paycheck			790	46		1,913	96
003	05/08	Hilltop Insurance	170	00				1,743	96
004	05/10	Tizzen Furniture	460	21				1,283	75
	05/11	ATM W/D	200	00				1,083	75
	05/12	Deposit, Fed Tax Refund			511	08		1,594	83
	05/13	Deposit, Paycheck			790	46		2,385	29
005	05/17	UniCard	416	28				1,969	01
	05/20	Deposit, Paycheck			790	46		2,759	47
006	05/27	Glenn's Auto Repair	109	74				2,649	73
007	05/28	Rhome Insurance Agency	689	17				1,960	56
008	05/28	Daily News (subscription)	142	20				1,818	36
	06/03	Deposit, State Tax Refund			86	20		1,904	56
009	06/04	Village Rentals	590	00				1,314	56

Integrated Project 3, continued

Step Two

Answer the questions that follow after you complete the reconciliation.

1. When you compared the bank statement and check register, you placed check marks in the ✓ column of the check register when the two forms agreed. There were four transactions you did not mark with a check mark in the check register. What are these unmarked transactions?

2. Check register items are marked only when they appear on a bank statement or after a correction for that transaction is made in the check register. Following this guideline, for which transactions may you now place a check mark in the √ column of the check register? Why?

3. What amount of interest was earned in May on the money on deposit in Tamyra's savings account?

4. Assume the annual interest rate remains at 1.5% and interest is compounded monthly. How much interest will Tamyra earn on her savings account in the month of June if she makes no other deposits or withdrawals from savings?

5. If Tamyra had placed her savings into a one-month certificate account that pays 4.2% annual interest, how much more could she have earned in interest on savings during May?

6. Assume that on May 1 Tamyra placed her $9,500 in savings into a one-year CD that pays 5.3% annual interest with a 3-month early withdrawal penalty. She withdrew $2,000 from the CD on November 1. What is the amount of the penalty?

7. **a.** How many electronic banking transactions did Tamyra have during May? **b.** Which electronic banking transaction did Tamyra use most frequently during May?

Lesson 4.1 *Promissory Notes*

Exercises

Ryce O'Fannon, a storeowner, needed money to purchase store equipment. She borrowed the money from Glen Palm Bank, signing the promissory note below. She pledged no collateral on the loan.

$ __15,600__	__Ocala, FL__	__April 25__	20 _02_

________Two years________ AFTER DATE__I__ PROMISE TO PAY TO

THE ORDER OF___Glen Palm Bank_______________________

__Fifteen thousand, six hundred and $\frac{no}{100}$__ ________________ DOLLARS

PAYABLE AT ___Glen Palm Bank_______________________

VALUE RECEIVED WITH INTEREST AT __12_ %

NO. _2079_ DUE _April 15_ 20 _04_ _______ Ryce O'Fannon

1. On the due date of the note shown above, how much did Ryce pay the Glen Palm Bank?

2. Ted Eisenstadt borrowed $5,600 from his bank for 4 months with interest at 9%. Ted paid the note in full on its due date. How much was the check he gave to the bank for payment?

3. Ahmed Yehda borrowed $8,000, signing a promissory note for $2\frac{1}{2}$ years at 15% interest. What was the amount due at maturity?

4. Bea Cruz signed a promissory note with a term of 3 years. The principal was $12,800 with interest at $12\frac{1}{2}$%. **a.** How much did Bea paid in interest on the note? **b.** On the maturity date, how much did Bea owe for principal and interest?

Lesson 4.1 *Promissory Notes*

Find the interest in each exercise below. (P = principal, R = rate, T = time)

	P	R	T	Interest		P	R	T	Interest
5.	$3,000	13%	3 yr		**9.**	$10,500	11.8%	9 mo	
6.	$8,500	8%	1.5 yr		**10.**	$4,250	7.5%	6 mo	
7.	$21,500	15%	0.5 yr		**11.**	$14,890	11.2%	3 mo	
8.	$1,680	9.5%	2 yr		**12.**	$6,270	6.5%	5 yr	

In each exercise, find the exact interest, to the nearest cent. (P = principal, R = rate, T = time)

	P	R	T	Interest		P	R	T	Interest
13.	$1,000	12%	60 days		**17.**	$150	8%	78 days	
14.	$22,500	9%	90 days		**18.**	$3,500	10%	210 days	
15.	$5,700	6.5%	120 days		**19.**	$2,800	14%	180 days	
16.	$560	11%	45 days		**20.**	$800	9.2%	30 days	

     Chapter 4 *Workbook*

Lesson 4.1 *Promissory Notes*

In each exercise, find the ordinary interest, to the nearest cent. (*P* = principal, *R* = rate, *T* = time)

	P	R	T	Interest		P	R	T	Interest
21.	$4,500	8%	90 days		**25.**	$6,000	12%	180 days	
22.	$10,200	9%	30 days		**26.**	$5,000	15%	40 days	
23.	$2,400	6%	60 days		**27.**	$1,000	9%	80 days	
24.	$1,800	18%	120 days		**28.**	$6,500	21%	50 days	

In each exercise, find the annual interest rate, to the nearest tenth percent. (*P* = principal, *T* = time, *I* = interest)

	P	T	I	Rate		P	T	I	Rate
29.	$6,000	9 mo	$315		**33.**	$6,400	4 mo	$192	
30.	$8,000	2 yr	$1,280		**34.**	$9,000	3 yr	$2,970	
31.	$4,200	3 mo	$89.25		**35.**	$2,400	2 yr	$576	
32.	$3,000	8 mo	$240		**36.**	$3,000	1.5 yr	$450	

Lesson 4.2 *Discounted Promissory Notes*

Exercises

1. Use these data to fill in the promissory note below: Face of note, $9,500; date, May 15; time, 3 months; payable to Village Bank; payable at Village Bank; interest, none; number, 19618; maker, Amalia Vadillo; collateral, 2003 Regent 6897041958318.

```
LOAN NO. __________              DATE ________________ 19 ________

LOAN AMOUNT $ __________ MATURITY DATE ________________ 19 ________
_______________________________________________________________

____________________________ AFTER DATE ________ PROMISE TO PAY TO

THE ORDER OF ___________________________________________________

_______________________________________________ DOLLARS
                    , and the obligation this agreement
PAYABLE AT _______________________ VALUE RECEIVED WITH INTEREST AT

THE RATE OF ________ % PER ANNUM, FOR VALUE RECEIVED, GIVING SAID BANK A

SECURITY INTEREST IN THIS COLLATERAL: ________________________

The rights ________ (am, are) giving said bank in this property
secures are defined on the reverse side of this note.

                              ____________________________
```

2. Amalia discounts the note above at her bank on May 15. The discount rate is 13%. What are the proceeds for which the bank will credit her account?

3. What was the true rate of interest Amalia paid on the note in exercise 2, to the nearest hundredth of a percent?

4. On April 12, Yi Sun found that he had overdrawn his checking account by $600. He then discounted at the bank his 3-month, non-interest-bearing note for $800 and had the proceeds put into his checking account. The bank's discount rate was 16%. What were the proceeds he received?

5. What was the true rate of interest Yi paid on the note in exercise 4, to the nearest hundredth of a percent?

Lesson 4.3 *Interest Tables*

Exercises

Use the interest table on page 145 of the textbook to solve exercises on this page. Find the interest for each promissory note in Exercises 1 – 10.

1. $550 @ 8% for 18 days

2. $8,590 @ 9.5% for 15 days

3. $2,100 @ 8.5% for 18 days

4. $9,300 @ 16% for 24 days

5. $5,000 @ 10.5% for 36 days

6. $3,800 @ 17.5% for 30 days

7. $11,000 @ 18.5% for 20 days

8. $6,280 @ 20% for 40 days

9. $21,500 @ 16.5% for 20 days

10. $1,200 @ 9% for 42 days

11. Andres Moya borrowed $3,000 on a note for 45 days with interest at 12%: **a.** What interest did Andres pay? **b.** What total amount did Andres owe when the note was due?

12. Ester Stein borrowed $21,000 for 60 days at 9% interest. When the note is due, how much does Ester owe?

13. Roman Medina needs to borrow $8,000 for 30 days. Bank A will lend him the money at 12% interest. Bank B will lend him the money at 12.5% interest. **a.** What is the interest cost at Bank A? **b.** What is the interest cost at Bank B? **c.** By borrowing at the lower interest cost, how much would Roman save?

Lesson 4.3 *Interest Tables*

14. On October 31, Sarah Willis borrowed $5,600 from the Vestal Central Bank. She gave the bank her 90-day note for that amount. The note was dated October 31, and the exact interest rate was 12%. **a.** Find the date of maturity for the note. **b.** How much did Sarah pay to the bank on the maturity date?

15. Oscar Leiberman needed to borrow money from his bank to remodel his home. To get the loan, he gave the bank his 120-day note for $32,500, dated April 20, bearing exact interest at $12\frac{1}{2}\%$. **a.** The note came due for payment on what date? **b.** Oscar paid the note on its due date by giving the bank a check for what amount?

The Winston Bank holds the notes below for loans to the people named in the "Maker" column. Show for each note the due date of the note, and the amount due at maturity. Use exact interest when the time is shown in days. Use the formula $I = PRT$ for your calculations.

	Maker	Face of Note	Date of Note	Time	Exact Interest Rate	Due Date	Amount Due at Maturity
16.	T. Alva	$6,800	Oct. 3	180 days	8%		
17.	G. Bohn	$2,500	Jan. 5	6 months	12%		
18.	B. Cone	$9,460	May 2	90 days	6%		
19.	E. Duff	$1,480	June 24	3 months	16%		
20.	R. Ellis	$14,000	Dec. 1	30 days	9.5%		
21.	V. Frank	$800	April 2	4 months	11%		
22.	W. Gull	$5,390	Nov. 11	60 days	10%		

Lesson 4.3 *Interest Tables*

23. On October 23, Carlos Cabrera borrowed $8,000 at 10.5% exact interest from the State Bank of Alton on a promissory note. He deposited 50 shares of Sintel Corporation common stock as collateral security. On January 17, he paid the note in full.

    a. Interest on the note is charged for ______ days.

    b. The amount of the interest is __________ .

    c. The amount that Lowe paid on January 17 in payment of the note and interest is _____________ .

During the year, the Trenton National Bank received payment for each of the twelve notes listed below. For each note, find the time of the note. Write your answers in the column headed "Time in Days."

	Maker	Date of Note	Date Paid	Time in Days
24.	Lynn	May 1	July 6	
25.	Makler	Jan. 15	Feb. 26	
26.	Nabe	Oct. 8	Dec. 3	
27.	Olds	July 5	Aug. 17	
28.	Parks	Mar. 2	Oct. 2	
29.	Quincy	Aug. 19	Nov. 8	
30.	Rolfe	Oct. 18	Feb. 15	
31.	Soto	Nov. 8	Jan. 16	
32.	Teng	April 2	Sept. 8	
33.	Uhler	Aug. 4	Feb. 22	
34.	Valdez	June 14	July 14	
35.	Waltz	Sept. 16	Dec. 24	

Lesson 4.4 *Installment Loans*

Exercises

1. The cash price of a home entertainment center is $4,500. It can be bought on the installment plan for $500 down and $137 a month for 36 months. **a.** What is the installment price of the home entertainment center? **b.** What is the finance charge?

2. You can buy a hand-held computer for $800 in cash or for $50 down and $39.25 each month for 24 months. **a.** What is the installment price of the computer? **b.** What is the finance charge? **c.** What is the percent by which the installment price exceeds the cash price?

Find the amount of equal monthly payment on each of the installment loans below.

	Installment Price	Down Payment	Number of Payments	Monthly Payment
3.	$916	$100	24	
4.	$2,350	$250	12	
5.	$470	$50	6	
6.	$12,488	$500	36	
7.	$1,565	$125	18	

Lesson 4.4 *Installment Loans*

Find the number of months it will take to repay the installment loans below.

	Installment Price	Down Payment	Monthly Payment	Number of Payments
8.	$24,800	$5,000	$330	
9.	$590	$50	$45	
10.	$3,580	$400	$132.50	
11.	$8,600	$500	$225	
12.	$236	$20	$18	

13. Gregorio Ruiz borrowed $3,000 on an 18-month simple interest installment loan at 12% interest. The monthly payments were $90.26. For the first month,

    a. What is the amount of interest?

    b. What amount is applied to the principal?

    c. What is the new balance after the first monthly payment?

14. Trish O'Hare signed a $1,800, 6-month simple interest installment loan at 8% interest. The monthly payments were $307.04. For the first three months,

    a. The amount of interest is ________; ________; ________.

    b. The amount applied to the principal is ________; ________; ________.

    c. The new balance after each of the first three monthly payments is ________; ________; ________.

Lesson 4.5 *Early Loan Repayments*

Exercises

Use the Finance Charge Refund Schedule on page 157 of the textbook to solve Exercises 1 – 7.

1. Antonio Rinaldi paid for a refrigerator with a 9-month Rule of 78 installment loan. The total finance charge for the loan was $240. He repaid the loan at the end of the third month. **a.** What was the amount of the unearned finance charges? **b.** What was the amount of the earned finance charges?

2. Camilya White paid back a 12-month, $3,000 Rule of 78 installment loan at the end of the sixth month. The total finance charge for the loan was $225. **a.** What was the amount of the unearned finance charges? **b.** What was the amount of earned finance charges?

Find the earned and unearned finance charges for the following Rule of 78 installment loans.

	Original Term of Loan	**Finance Charge**	**Loan Paid at End of**	**Earned Finance Charges**	**Unearned Finance Charges**
3.	6 months	$360	3 months		
4.	21 months	$270	9 months		
5.	12 months	$130	6 months		
6.	18 months	$250	12 months		
7.	15 months	$300	6 months		

8. Eva repays a 12-month, $4,500 Rule of 78 installment loan on the day that the ninth monthly payment is due. The loan's total finance charge is $396. The monthly installment payments were $408. What amount does Eva pay when she pays off the loan?

9. Rudy has an 18-month, $7,600 Rule of 78 installment loan with a total finance charge of $896. The monthly installment payments are $472. He repays the loan on the due date of the twelfth monthly payment. What amount does Rudy need to pay off the loan?

Lesson 4.6 *Annual Percentage Rates*

Exercises

1. Trudy Costello borrowed $1,600 on a loan with a finance charge of $156. What is the finance charge per $100 of the amount financed?

For Exercises 2 – 5, use the table on page 162 of the textbook to find the APR.

2. Jim Morgan borrows $5,200 from the loan department of his bank. Jim repays the loan in 15 equal installments of $379.90. **a.** Find the total amount that Jim repaid to the bank. **b.** What is the total finance charge for the loan? **c.** What is the finance charge per $100 of the amount financed? **d.** What is the annual percentage rate?

3. Maria Cruz borrows $600 from a loan company. She must repay the loan in 6 equal installments of $104. **a.** Find the total amount to be repaid. **b.** What is the total finance charge on the loan? **c.** What is the finance charge per $100 of the amount financed? **d.** What is the annual percentage rate?

4. Tyrone Lacy repays a loan of $4,000 in 12 monthly installments of $360 each. **a.** Find the total amount repaid. **b.** What is the finance charge on the loan? **c.** What is the finance charge per $100 of the amount financed? **d.** What is the annual percentage rate?

5. Sissy Marshall gets a personal loan at a bank for $3,500 that she repays in 15 equal monthly installments of $253.75. **a.** Find the total amount she repays. **b.** What is the total finance charge on the loan? **c.** What is the finance charge per $100 of the amount financed? **d.** What is the annual percentage rate?

                                                    Chapter 4 *Workbook*

Lesson 4.6 *Annual Percentage Rates*

Use the table below to find the APR for Exercises 6 – 10.

No of Payments	Annual Percentage Rate										
	14.00	14.25	14.50	14.75	15.00	15.25	15.50	15.75	16.00	17.00	18.00
	(Finance Charge per $100 of Amount Financed)										
6	4.12	4.2	4.27	4.35	4.42	4.49	4.57	4.64	4.72	5.02	5.32
12	7.74	7.89	8.03	8.17	8.31	8.45	8.59	8.74	8.88	9.45	10.02
18	11.45	11.66	11.87	12.08	12.29	12.5	12.72	12.93	13.14	13.99	14.85
20	12.70	12.93	13.17	13.41	13.64	13.88	14.11	14.35	14.59	15.54	16.49
24	15.23	15.51	15.80	16.08	16.37	16.65	16.94	17.22	17.51	18.66	19.82
30	19.10	19.45	19.81	20.17	20.54	20.90	21.26	21.62	21.99	23.45	24.92
36	23.04	23.48	23.92	24.35	24.8	25.24	25.68	26.12	26.57	28.35	30.15

6. A small boat can be bought for $3,000 cash or on the installment plan by paying $300 down and $108 a month for 30 months. **a.** What is the installment price of the boat? **b.** What is the finance charge? **c.** What is the amount financed? **d.** What is the finance charge per $100 of the amount financed? **e.** What is the annual percentage rate?

For each of these installment purchases, show the total monthly payments, installment price, the finance charge, the amount financed, the finance charge per $100 of the amount financed, and the annual percentage rate.

	Cash Price	Down Pay-ment	Monthly Payments			Install-ment Price	Finance Charge	Amt. Financed	Finance Charge per $100	APR
			No.	Each	Total					
7.	$400	$40	30	$14.40						
8.	$600	$75	12	$47.60						
9.	$280	$28	6	$43.89						
10.	$1,400	$140	36	$44.03						

Lesson 4.7 *Credit Card Costs*

Exercises

1. Clara Gorbea's March credit card statement had a previous balance of $185.86, new purchases of $216.39, a membership fee of $25, a finance charge of $4.76, and a payment of $200. What was her new balance?

2. The credit card statement of Fujio Mori for October listed a previous balance of $649.15, new purchases of $428.95, a payment of $500, a finance charge of $9.72, and a late fee of $20. What was his new balance?

3. Ti Barlow checked his credit card statement and found that a sales slip dated 5/3 for $121.56 was posted as $125.16. He also found that a purchase for $75.92 dated 5/19 was unauthorized. The new balance on his statement was $541.33. What is the correct new balance?

4. Lisa Valente found a sales slip for $82.59 on her credit card statement that was unauthorized. She also found that a sales slip for $24.68 had been listed as $42.68. If the new balance on her statement was $329.76, what is her correct new balance?

5. Yvonda Wether's credit card statement included a sales slip for $52.96 that was unauthorized. She also found that a sales slip for $31.62 had been listed as $33.62. The new balance shown on her statement was $210.45. What is her correct new balance?

Lesson 4.7 *Credit Card Costs*

6. The credit card statement of Peter Sayles for November 30 showed a previous balance of $481.47; a payment of $300 on 11/2; and new purchases of $68.99 on 11/10, $45 on 11/15, $72.75 on 11/17; and a new balance of $368.21 for the month. Peter found on checking his sales slips that the slip dated 11/10 was actually for $58.99 and that there was no slip dated 11/17 for $72.75. He was certain this purchase was unauthorized by him. What is Peter's correct new balance?

7. Tammy Janes started a MasterTerm credit card in January. She paid a membership fee of $35 and a balance transfer fee of $27 when she moved the balance of her old card to her new card. During the year, she paid these finance charges: Feb., $1.86; Mar., $5.32; July, $8.42; Nov., $5.28. What was Tammy's total annual cost of the card?

8. Ricardo Brock's credit card statement for July included a membership fee of $20, a late fee of $25, a finance charge of $9.65, and an over-the-limit fee of $12. What was the total cost of the card to Ricardo in July?

9. Sondra Koropolos signed up for a new credit card in January. She paid a membership fee of $75 and a balance transfer fee of $27 when she moved the balance of her old card to her new card. During the year, she paid these finance charges: Jan., $4.35; April. $3.18; Aug., $5.29; Oct., $1.28. Find the total annual cost of the card to Sondra.

10. The credit card statements for Dick Tomer for the year showed: membership fee, $35; three late fees of $23; and an average finance charge of $2.75 a month. Find the total annual cost of the card to Dick.

Lesson 4.8 *Credit Card Finance Charges*

Exercises

1. Laura West's credit card company uses an APR of 17% figured on the previous balance. The previous balance on Laura's credit card statement for November was $308.88. The statement also showed new purchases and fees of $327.74, and payments and credits of $350 in November. **a.** What is Laura's finance charge for November? **b.** Find her new balance.

2. Dirk Gooden has a credit card that charges an APR of 20% on his previous balance. Dirk's April statement showed: previous balance, $109.70; new purchases, $231.80; fees, $75; payments, $200; purchase return, $45.99. **a.** What is Dirk's finance charge for April? **b.** Find his new balance.

3. A credit card company issues a statement listing the following: previous balance, $461.88; purchases, $296.89; fees, $65; payments, $400; credits, $25. The credit card company uses an APR of 12% and the adjusted balance method of computing finance charges. **a.** What is the finance charge for the month? **b.** Find the new balance.

4. Ana Melendez's credit card statement lists a previous balance of $759.86, new purchases and fees of $420.78, and payments and credits of $450. Ana's card company charges an APR of 14% on the adjusted balance. **a.** What is Ana's finance charge? **b.** Find Ana's new balance.

Lesson 4.8 *Credit Card Finance Charges*

5. When Karla Morjic opened her March credit card statement she found these items shown: 3/1, previous balance, $245.89; 3/7, purchase, $106.99; 3/10, purchase, $75.78; 3/25, payment, $200. Karla's card company uses a 1.8% monthly periodic rate and the average daily balance method. **a.** What is Karla's finance charge for March? **b.** Find Karla's new balance.

6. On her September credit card statement, Taffyta Hackman found these items: 9/1, previous balance, $319.29; 9/11, purchase, $105.89; 9/15, purchase, $67.18; 9/24, payment, $175. The card company uses the average daily balance method and a daily periodic rate of 0.056%. **a.** What is Taffyta's finance charge for September? **b.** Find Taffyta's new balance.

7. Ying borrowed $350 for 60 days from his credit card company using a cash advance. The company charged a daily finance charge of 0.052%. What was Ying's finance charge for the loan?

8. Alicia used a $250 cash advance from her credit card company to get cash while on a trip. The company charges a daily finance fee of 0.047%. She repaid the advance plus the finance fee 40 days later. What amount did Alicia repay the company?

9. Tony uses a credit card company that charges a yearly membership fee of $25, $28 for a late fee, and a daily finance charge of 0.055% on all cash advances. Last month, Tony was charged for his annual membership fee, a late fee, and a $300 cash advance that he borrowed for 30 days. What was the total amount that the credit card company charged Tony?

Term Puzzler

Complete the crossword puzzle below. Some answers are two words placed together without space between them.

Across

1. Security for a loan
5. Money borrowed using a credit card is called a cash _____
6. Percent of interest paid
7. Credit card balance method that subtracts payments and credits in this month from balance at end of last month
8. Time period given to pay credit card balance in full before finance charges are added
9. Type of note used when borrowing money
12. Events recorded on credit card statements
14. _____ of 78 installment loan
18. Money paid to use other peoples' money
19. Monthly periodic rate is the APR divided by _____
20. Bank _____ is subtracted from a loan in advance

Down

2. Method of calculating interest that uses a 365-day year
3. Type of fee paid for missing payment date
4. A daily balance method for finding credit card balances
7. Annual percentage rate
9. Amount received after bank discount is subtracted
10. A method of calculating interest that uses a 360-day year
11. Type of loan repaid in part payments
13. Part of purchase price paid up front is called down _____
15. Difference between installment price and cash price is the finance _____
16. That part of finance charge lender must refund when loan is repaid early is called _____ interest
17. Most you can spend using your credit card without paying a special fee is the credit _____

Integrated Project 4

Directions Read through the entire project before you begin doing any work.

Carmen and Leon Espino have been shopping for a folding camper trailer they can use for family trips. They have shopped carefully for the trailer and think they have found the right trailer and dealer for their needs. They bargained for a cash price of $6,500 for the trailer.

The Espinos also shopped carefully to find the best deal for borrowing the money they will need to buy the trailer. They found four sources for the funds they need: the dealer, their bank, their credit union, and a special low-interest rate credit card. The information they have gathered about each loan follows. Answer the questions about each loan offer and then compare the offers.

The Dealer's Offer: Marsh Camping Equipment, Inc., has offered the Espinos an installment plan with these terms: 10% down and the remainder to be paid in 24 equal payments of $283.65 each. Under this plan,

1. The amount financed is __________.

2. The installment price of the trailer is __________.

3. The total finance charge is __________.

4. The installment price of the trailer is _______% greater, to the nearest tenth percent, than the cash price.

5. Using the table below, the annual percentage rate for the dealer's offer is ______%.

No of Payments	Annual Percentage Rate										
	14.00	14.25	14.50	14.75	15.00	15.25	15.50	15.75	16.00	17.00	18.00
	(Finance Charge per $100 of Amount Financed)										
6	4.12	4.2	4.27	4.35	4.42	4.49	4.57	4.64	4.72	5.02	5.32
12	7.74	7.89	8.03	8.17	8.31	8.45	8.59	8.74	8.88	9.45	10.02
18	11.45	11.66	11.87	12.08	12.29	12.5	12.72	12.93	13.14	13.99	14.85
20	12.70	12.93	13.17	13.41	13.64	13.88	14.11	14.35	14.59	15.54	16.49
24	15.23	15.51	15.80	16.08	16.37	16.65	16.94	17.22	17.51	18.66	19.82
30	19.10	19.45	19.81	20.17	20.54	20.90	21.26	21.62	21.99	23.45	24.92
36	23.04	23.48	23.92	24.35	24.8	25.24	25.68	26.12	26.57	28.35	30.15

    Chapter 4 *Workbook*

Integrated Project 4, continued

The Bank's Offer: The Watertown National Bank has offered the Espinos the promissory note shown below. The Espinos will have to sign the promissory note and pledge the trailer as collateral. The bank will discount their note at 12%. The entire amount is due one year later. No monthly payments are required.

LOAN NO. __40839__   DATE __June 1__ 20 __03__

LOAN AMOUNT $ __7,386.36__   MATURITY DATE __June 1__ 20 __04__

________ *One year* ________ AFTER DATE __We__ PROMISE TO PAY TO

THE ORDER OF ________ *Watertown National Bank* ________

Seven thousand, three hundred eighty-six and $\frac{36}{100}$ ________ DOLLARS

PAYABLE AT ____ *Watertown National Bank* ____ VALUE RECEIVED WITH INTEREST AT

THE RATE OF __none__ % PER ANNUM, FOR VALUE RECEIVED, GIVING SAID BANK A

SECURITY INTEREST IN THIS COLLATERAL: __Collateral, Seneca Camping Trailer__

The rights __We__ (am, are) giving said bank in this property, and the obligations this agreement secures are defined on the reverse side of this note.

________ *Tina Espinos* ________   ________ *Marco Espinos* ________

Under this plan,

6. The total amount of bank discount the Espinos will pay is _________.

7. The proceeds the Espinos will receive from this note are _________.

8. The true rate of interest on the note, to the nearest tenth of a percent, is ______%.

9. The total amount of money the Espinos will pay for the trailer is _________.

10. The total amount the Espinos will pay for the trailer, to the nearest tenth of a percent, is ______% greater than the cash price.

     Chapter 4 *Workbook*

Integrated Project 4, *continued*

The Credit Union's Offer: Their credit union has offered the Espinos these terms: A $6,500, two-year loan with interest on the unpaid balance at the monthly rate of 1%. They must make monthly payments of $305.98. The Espinos must also sign a promissory note for the loan and pledge the trailer as collateral.

11. Complete the monthly payment schedule shown at the right. Because of rounding, the last payment must be adjusted so that the Espinos pay no more than the original principal of $6,500 and the interest due. The schedule has been partially completed for you.

Under this plan,

12. The total financed price of the trailer is

    __________.

13. The total finance charges are __________.

14. The total installment plan price of the trailer is __________% greater, to the nearest tenth of a percent, than the cash price.

15. The annual rate of interest charged is _____%.

UBC Credit Union				
Loan Payment Schedule				
Leon and Carmen Espino				
Month	Unpaid Balance	Principal Payment	Monthly Interest	Total Payment
1	6,500.00	240.98	65.00	305.98
2	6,259.02	243.39	62.59	305.98
3	6,015.63	245.82	60.16	305.98
4	5,769.81	248.28	57.70	305.98
5	5,521.53	250.76	55.22	305.98
6	5,270.77	253.27	52.71	305.98
7	5,017.50	255.80	50.18	305.98
8	4,761.70	258.36	47.62	305.98
9	4,503.34	260.95	45.03	305.98
10	4,242.39	263.56	42.42	305.98
11	3,978.83	266.19	39.79	305.98
12	3,712.64	268.85	37.13	305.98
13				
14				
15				
16				
17				
18				
19				
20				
21				
22				
23				
24	302.91	302.91	3.03	305.94
Totals				

Integrated Project 4, continued

The Credit Card Offer: The Espinos have just received a new credit card offer that lets them charge up to $10,000 on their card. The card offers a 3% annual percentage rate for the first three months. After that, an 18% annual percentage rate is charged. Finance charges are based on the previous balance. If they buy the trailer using the credit card, no down payment is required. The Espinos will not make any other purchases with the card until the trailer is paid off. The first payment is due on July 1. They plan to pay $313.10 each month to the credit card company until the $6,500 charge is eliminated.

16. Complete the chart showing the monthly finance charge, total payment, and new balance. Because of rounding, the last payment must be adjusted so that the Espinos pay no more than the original balance of $6,500 and the interest due.

17. The total credit card price of the trailer is __________.

18. The total finance charges are

    __________.

19. The total credit card price is ______% greater, (nearest tenth), than the cash price.

Comparing the offers,

20. Which offer, other than the bank's offer, provides the lowest monthly payment? Why? ____________

    ____

21. Which offer results in the lowest price for the trailer? ____________

22. How much money would be saved by taking the offer with the lowest total price rather than the offer with the highest total price?

Payment Number	Unpaid Balance	Planned Principal Payment	Monthly Interest	Total Payment
1	6,500.00	296.85	16.25	313.10
2	6,203.15	297.59	15.51	313.10
3				313.10
4				313.10
5	5,378.23	232.43	80.67	313.10
6	5,145.80	235.91	77.19	313.10
7	4,909.89	239.45	73.65	313.10
8	4,670.44	243.04	70.06	313.10
9	4,427.40	246.69	66.41	313.10
10	4,180.71	250.39	62.71	313.10
11	3,930.32	254.15	58.95	313.10
12	3,676.17	257.96	55.14	313.10
13				313.10
14				313.10
15				313.10
16				313.10
17				313.10
18				313.10
19				313.10
20				313.10
21				313.10
22				313.10
23				313.10
24	312.09	312.09	4.68	316.77
Totals				

23. Which offer do you think the Espinos should take? Why? _________________________________

    ____

Name ____ Date ___________

Lesson 5.1 *Sales Tax*

Exercises

1. The form below shows the item price and state and city sales tax rates for five items. Calculate the sales tax and total price of each item. Write each amount in the proper column in the form.

Item	Price	State Sales Tax Rate	City Sales Tax Rate	Sales Tax	Total Price
a.	$539	5.00%	1.50%		
b.	$35.79	4.50%	2.30%		
c.	$1,078.88	3.40%	2.00%		
d.	$251.09	8.00%	1.25%		
e.	$5.19	4.20%	2.25%		

2. The form below shows the taxable price and nontaxable price of five purchases and the state and city sales tax rates. Calculate the sales tax and total price of each item. Write each amount in the proper column in the form.

Item	Taxable Item Price	Nontaxable Item price	State Sales Tax Rate	City Sales Tax Rate	Sales Tax	Total Price
a.	$160.88	$42.18	3.50%	--		
b.	$308.99	$79.39	7.50%	--		
c.	$2,487.12	$411.18	6.25%	1.25%		
d.	$803.15	$189.59	2.50%	2.25%		
e.	$89.29	$315.88	3.75%	3.45%		

Chapter 5 *Workbook*

Lesson 5.2 *Sales Receipts*

Exercises

1. Complete the sales slip below.

THE MODEL SHOP		98 Woodneigh Road, Pekin, IL 61554-0098
CALL 309-555-1289	SOLD TO:	Alicia Varney
FROM 8 a.m. to 5 p.m. daily, except Sunday	STREET	4005 Clarmet St.
DATE Aug. 20 --	CITY, STATE, ZIP	Pekin, IL 61554-4005

SOLD BY I.S.	CASH ✓	CHARGE	C.O.D.	DELIVER BY Taken

QUANTITY	DESCRIPTION	UNIT PRICE	AMOUNT
2	Telephone stand kits	28.98	
3 boxes	Mixed sandpaper	2.75	
4 doz.	1" Wood screws	2.98	
4	Carrier models	18.89	
3	Bottles of wood glue	2.98	
CRAFTS ARE FUN! START A PROJECT TODAY.	SUBTOTAL		
	SALES TAX	6.25%	
	TOTAL		

2. Check each calculation on the sales slip below. If there is an error, cross out the incorrect amount and write the correct amount to the right of the incorrect amount.

TI'S CYCLE CENTER		2708 Valley Road, Albuquerque, NM 87114-4094
CALL 505-348-1888	SOLD TO:	Ben Murtz
FROM 8 a.m. to 10 p.m.	STREET	905 Stueben St.
DATE June 1 20__ --	CITY, STATE, ZIP	Albuquerque, NM 87107-9897

SOLD BY T.M.	CASH	CHARGE ✓	C.O.D.	DELIVER BY Taken

QUANTITY	DESCRIPTION	UNIT PRICE	AMOUNT
2	All terrain bicycles	139.99	279.98
2	Saddlebags	22.77	45.54
8 pr.	Athletic socks	5.98	47.84
3	Ti s Cycle Center T-shirts	8.88	26.64
2	Reflectors	4.89	9.87
MOUNTAIN BIKETHON EVENT EVERY MAY, THIS YEAR JOIN US!	SUBTOTAL		409.87
	SALES TAX	5%	20.49
	TOTAL		430.36

Lesson 5.2 *Sales Receipts*

3. Check each calculation on the sales slip below. If there is an error, cross out the incorrect amount and write the correct amount to the right of the incorrect amount.

OLLIE'S OVEN 2291 Pike Drive, Peoria, IL 61609-2454				
CALL 309-446-1818 SOLD TO: *Tyrone Brown*				
DA Nov. 1 20___ STREET: 9797 Union St.				
CITY, STATE, ZIP *Peoria, IL* 61604-6755				
SOLD BY A.T.	CASH ✓	CHARGE		
QUANTITY	DESCRIPTION		UNIT PRICE	AMOUNT
1 doz.	Hard rolls		2.29	2.29
3	Loaves whole wheat bread	1.22	3.66	
4 doz.	Croissant rolls		6.99	27.96
5	Loaves pumpernickel bread	1.19	5.95	
1	Loaf rye bread		1.28	1.28
EVERYTHING BAKED FRESH EVERY DAY!	SUBTOTAL			41.14
	SALES TAX		6.25%	2.75
	TOTAL			43.89

4. Check each calculation on the sales slip below. If there is an error, cross out the incorrect amount and write the correct amount to the right of the incorrect amount.

PRETTIE PARTIES 56 Broad Street, Pacific, MO 63069-6518			
CALL 314-863-1245 SOLD TO: Lonnie McNamara			
DATE Jan. 5 20___ STREET: 2407 Lee Ave.			
CITY, STATE, ZIP St. Louis, MO 63123-6518			
SOLD BY B.L.	CASH ✓	CHARGE	
QUANTITY	DESCRIPTION	UNIT PRICE	AMOUNT
3 boxes	Cards	7.36	22.08
5 doz.	Party napkins	2.99	14.95
3 decks	Playing cards	5.63	16.89
2	Table covers	8.15	16.30
24	Party hats	2.34	56.16
GIFTS FOR EVERY OCCASION	SUBTOTAL		126.36
	SALES TAX	6.075%	7.68
	TOTAL		134.04

Lesson 5.3   *Unit Prices*

Exercises

1. You can buy 1 set of 6 Cottonsoft bath towels for $69.99 or 2 sets of 3 Bathtyme bath towels for $35.59 per set. **a.** What brand of towels costs less per towel? **b.** How much less per towel, to the nearest tenth of a cent?

2. Store A sells a package of 4 twin bed sheets for $31.95. Store B sells a similar quality sheet in a package of 6 for $49.99. **a.** Which store sells the sheets for less per sheet? **b.** How much less per sheet, to the nearest tenth of a cent?

3. A supermarket sells 4, 1 lb. cans of Colombian coffee for $15.99. A corner grocery store sells the same brand of coffee on sale for 3, 2 lb. cans for $24.99. **a.** Which store sells the coffee for the least price per pound? **b.** How much less per pound, to the nearest tenth of a cent?

4. Find the price of one unit of each item.

	Qty.	Item	Total Price	Price of One Unit
a.	2	Battery charger	$79.99	
b.	4	Rechargeable batteries	24.98	
c.	3	Bottles of pain reliever	2.99	
d.	8	Paper gift bags	3.89	
e.	4	Boxes of cold tablets	4.29	
f.	8	Videotapes	19.99	
g.	3	Printer cartridges	76.99	

Lesson 5.4 *Comparative Shopping*

Exercises

1. The price of whole milk in a gallon jug is $2.99. The same milk in quart containers is $1.19. How much do you save by buying milk in the gallon jug?

2. Three music CDs are regularly priced at an area store for $8.99 each. If you buy them from an online store, you pay $7.89 plus a shipping and handling fee of $3.15. **a.** Which store offers the better deal? **b.** How much better?

3. As an introductory offer, a cable TV company will install the cable service free and charge you $38 a month for the first year's service. The regular price is $55 for installation and $43 a month for the service fee. **a.** If you take the introductory offer, how much will you save in the first year? **b.** What percent of the regular monthly service fee, to the nearest tenth percent, is the savings on the monthly service fee?

4. A small motel wants to buy 9 table lamps for some of its guest rooms that it is remodeling. Each lamp is priced at $76.95 if from 1 to 5 are bought, and $68.95 if more than 5 are bought at one time. **a.** How much will the company save by buying 9 lamps all at once instead of nine lamps, one at a time? **b.** What is the percent saved by buying all nine lamps now, to the nearest tenth percent?

5. Paulson's Hardware Store is selling a room air cleaner for $69.85, with a factory rebate of $12. Big Mart is selling a similar air cleaner for $59.89, with a discount of 10%. **a.** What is the net cost of the air cleaner: from Paulson's? **b.** from Big Mart's? **c.** If you bought the air cleaner from the less expensive store, how much would you save?

Lesson 5.4 *Comparative Shopping*

6. Janyce Reece estimates that it will take 3 hours to sand her living room and dining room floors and another 2.5 hours to sand the floors in the two bedrooms in her house. She can rent a floor sander for $3 an hour, $7 a half day, or $12 for a full day. If she does all the rooms in one day, find: **a.** the cost using the hourly rate; **b.** the cost using the half-day rate; **c.** How much will Janice save by using the least expensive rental option rather than the most expensive rental option.

7. The Chess Club of Martinsville High School wants to rent a hotdog steamer to sell hotdogs at the next school football game. They estimate that they will need the steamer for 4 hours. They can rent the steamer for $10 a day, $6 a half day, or $2.75 an hour. **a.** What rental rate will be the most expensive? **b.** What rental rate will be the least expensive? **c.** How much will be saved by choosing the least rather than the most expensive rate?

8. A homeowner can rent a garden tiller for $32 a day or purchase a used tiller from the same company for $249.99. **a.** If she rents the tiller for two days twice a year, what would be the annual cost? **b.** At the day rate, find the number of days the homeowner could rent the tiller before the cost of renting exceeded the cost of buying, to the nearest whole day.

9. Ben Stiller can rent a lawn thatcher for $8.50 an hour or $39 for a full day from Johnson Rentals. Sylvan Garden Market sells the same thatcher new for $549.95. **a.** If Ben estimates that the thatcher will be needed for 6 hours, once each year, find the cost of renting by the hour. **b.** How much will Ben save by renting it for the whole day rather than by the hour? **c.** How many days would Ben have to rent the thatcher, to the nearest whole day, before the cost of renting it at the day rate exceeds the purchase cost?

10. In your town, bicycles rent for $45 a week or $8.75 a day. **a.** By renting for a whole week instead of one day at a time, how much would you save? **b.** If the same bicycle can be bought for $179, find the number of weeks, to the nearest whole week, it would take before the cost of weekly rentals would be more than buying?

Lesson 5.5 *Personal Internet Access*

Exercises

1. Tryg Valencia purchases a digital subscriber line connection from his telephone company. The company charges a $75 installation fee, $65 for a network connection card for his computer, and a monthly online access fee of $49.95 for an unlimited connection. Tryg also buys antivirus software for $29.89 and firewall software for $19.99. What is Tryg's total cost to connect to the Internet for the first year?

2. Regalnet, an ISP, charges a set-up fee of $25 for a dial-up connection to the Internet. Access fees are $15 per month for 100 hours per month of connect time and $25 per month for an unlimited connection for one whole year. A two-year unlimited connection costs $575. **a.** By paying for unlimited service on a 2-year basis instead of a monthly basis, how much will you save? **b.** By subscribing to a limited access connection for one year, how much will you save over the cost of a one-year, unlimited connection?

3. Find the time it takes to transfer each of the files below, to the nearest tenth of a second.

File	Connection Speed	Size of File	Time in Seconds
a.	56 kbps	34 KB	
b.	128 kbps	1.4 MB	
c.	256 kbps	4.5 MB	
d.	512 kbps	76 KB	
e.	768 kbps	15.6 MB	

4. Jamie Kirk changes from a dial-up Internet connection rated at 28 kbps to a cable connection rated at 512 kbps. How many times faster than the old connection is the new connection, to the nearest whole number?

Chapter 5 *Workbook*

Term Puzzler

Directions Each group of scrambled letters can be sorted to spell a word or phrase. Unscramble the letters to form a word or phrase. Then sort the letters in boxes to form a key word.

a. Sort the scrambled letters below.

1. asles xta

   —   —   —   —   —   □   —   —

2. nextosine

   —   —   —   —   □   —   —   —   —

3. lonine

   —   —   —   —   —   □

4. bottalus

   —   —   —   □   —   —   —   —

5. niut cripe

   —   —   □   —   —   —   —   —   —

6. secsac efe

   —   —   —   □   —   —   —   □   —

7. wonaddlo

   —   —   —   □   —   —   —   —

8. lawrefil

   —   —   □   —   —   —   —   —

9. teby

   —   —   □

10. charke

   □   —   —   —   —   —

b. The key words are _______________________________.

Integrated Project 5

Directions Read through the entire project before you begin doing any work.

Step One

Lisa and Juan Guzman have just been married. They plan to move to a small apartment in Mercuson,
Alabama, where they work. The couple needs to move the furniture Juan has in his three-room apartment
to their apartment. Juan called two different moving companies to get estimates on the cost of moving.
The Levy Moving Company said that Juan had 4,100 lb. of furniture to move at a cost of $8.45 per
hundred lb. The Kairphul Moving Company said that they would do the job for a flat fee of $378.

1. What are the moving costs to be charged by Levy Moving Co.?

2. Which company offers the better price?

3. How much less does the better price cost?

Step Two

The Guzmans wish to clean the wall-to-wall rugs in their apartment before moving in. They estimate
that they can clean the rugs in five hours. They can rent a carpet cleaner from BadBoys Hardware for
$9 for the first 4 hours per day and $1.50 for each added hour. The rental rate for the same cleaner is
$12.99 for a full day. They can also buy a similar machine for $269, or have Floor-Brite Cleaning
Service do the job for $149.99.

4. If they rent the carpet cleaner for the time estimated, is half-day or full-day renting cheaper, and by how
   much?

5. If they rent by the cheaper method, how much will they save over Floor-Brite's Cleaning Service's price?

                                                    Chapter 5 *Workbook*

Integrated Project 5, continued

6. For how many days, to the nearest tenth day, can they rent the carpet cleaner before the daily rental cost is more than the cleaner's price?

Step Three

Lisa buys curtains and other items for the new apartment from the Value Department Store. The incomplete sales slip for her purchase is shown below. Complete the sales slip. Use a state sales tax rate of 4%.

VALUE DEPARTMENT STORE	3089 Melvane St., Mercuson, AL 36606-3089
205-555-0586	SOLD TO: Lisa Guzman
SINCE 1878	STREET 2238 Vescher Place, Apt. 6a
	CITY, STATE, ZIP Mercuson, AL 36609-1088

SOLD BY MS ✓	CASH ✓	CHARGE	C.O.D.	DELIVER BY Taken

QUANTITY	DESCRIPTION	UNIT PRICE	AMOUNT
3	Throw rug	11.99	
1	Bath tub mat	3.99	
6	Pairs, curtains	19.89	
6	Curtain rod kits	11.29	

MOBILE S OLDEST
AND FINEST
DEPARTMENT STORE

SUBTOTAL	
SALES TAX 4%	
TOTAL	

Step Four

Lisa and Juan also set up an office area in the smaller of their two bedrooms. They decide to connect Lisa's personal computer to the Internet using a cable connection from American Cable Co. American sells them the following hardware: a cable modem for $75 and a network connection card for $75, both of which are subject to the state sales tax of 4%. It also charges them $75 to install the cable, cable modem, and network card. State sales taxes are not levied on labor in Alabama. The Guzmans decide to take the 512 kbps unlimited Internet access service for $29.95 a month.

7. What is the total cost of the Internet hardware and its installation?

8. What is the total cost of American's Internet access service for the first year?

     Chapter 5 *Workbook*

Lesson 6.1 *Borrowing to Buy a Home*

Exercises

1. Anna wants to buy a home priced at $67,000. She will need to make a down payment of 15% and estimates closing costs of 2.8% of the purchase price. **a.** Anna will need what amount for the down payment? **b.** What amount will Anna need for the closing costs?

2. The Ayers are buying a used mobile home for $32,000. **a.** What amount do they need if they want to make a down payment of 30% of the purchase price? **b.** What amount are closing costs if they are estimated to be 3.2% of the purchase price? **c.** What is the total amount of cash needed by the Ayers to buy the mobile home?

3. Jason Searcy buys a condominium for $96,200. He makes a 5% down payment, and pays these closing costs: property survey, $315; insect inspection, $190; legal fees, $525; and title insurance, $225. **a.** What is the down payment amount? **b.** What are the total closing costs? **c.** What is the total cash amount needed to buy the condominium?

4. The Mintos bought a home for $234,000. They made a 10% down payment and paid these closing costs: legal fees, $620; survey costs, $275; title insurance, $350; loan origination fees, $1,280; home inspection, $475. **a.** How much was the down payment the Mintos ? **b.** How much did they pay in closing costs? **c.** The closing costs were what percent of the purchase price, to the nearest tenth percent.

5. Agnes Corcoran bought a $125,000 home. She made a 12% down payment and borrowed the rest on a 25-year, 8.8% fixed-rate mortgage. Her monthly mortgage payment was $908.10. **a.** How much was the down payment Agnes made? **b.** How much did she borrow on the mortgage? **c.** What is the total amount of the monthly payments Agnes expects to pay over the life of the loan? **d.** What is the amount of interest Agnes will pay over the 25-year loan term?

Lesson 6.1 *Borrowing to Buy a Home*

6. The Caverleys bought a home for $162,500. They made a 5% down payment and borrowed the rest on a 7.4%, 30-year fixed rate mortgage. Their monthly payment was $1,068.86. **a.** How much was the down payment they made? **b.** How much was the amount of their mortgage? **c.** What was the total amount of their monthly payments over 30 years? **d.** What was the amount of interest they paid over the life of the loan?

7. Basil Jacobs bought a house and signed an agreement with a bank for an $84,000, 25-year mortgage at 9.1%. The monthly mortgage payments are $710.69. Basil delayed buying the house for six months because interest rates had been falling. Had Basil bought the house 6 months ago his mortgage would have been at a 9.45% interest rate with monthly mortgage payments of $730.99. **a.** What is the difference between the two monthly payments for a month? **b.** What is the difference between the two monthly payments for a year? **c.** If Basil bought the house six months earlier, how much more would he have paid in interest over the life of the loan?

8. Tamyra Glover needs to borrow $96,000 to buy a house. Freedom Capital will give her a 7.5%, 25-year mortgage with monthly payments of $709.43. Asden Bank & Trust will give her a 30-year mortgage at the same rate and with monthly payments $671.25. **a.** If Tamyra takes the 25-year loan, her monthly payment will be how much more than with the 30-year loan? **b.** The total interest paid over the life of the 25-year loan will be how much less than with the 30-year loan.

9. Sebastian DeVries' old mortgage has a monthly payment of $997.73. The monthly payment on a new mortgage will be $845.32. To refinance the old mortgage, Sebastian must pay $871 in closing costs and $615 in prepayment penalties. How much less will he pay in the first year with the new mortgage?

10. The Clark's old mortgage payment was $855.78 a month. Their new monthly payment is $719.40. To refinance their old mortgage, they had to pay $714 in closing costs and $390 in prepayment penalties. What was the net amount they paid less in the first year with the new mortgage?

Lesson 6.2 *Renting or Owning a Home*

Exercises

1. The Montoyas want to buy a condominium. They estimate that their expenses in the first year will be: mortgage interest, $4,964; real estate taxes, $1,795; insurance, $386; association fees, $840; depreciation, $1,781; maintenance, $300; utilities, $1,200; lost income on cash invested, $525. They also estimate they will save $1,400 in income taxes because of increased tax deductions. **a.** What were the total expenses of condo ownership for the first year? **b.** What was the net cost of owning the condo in the first year?

2. Willard and Betsy Hogan want to buy a home. They will pay mortgage interest in the first year of $9,200. Annual property taxes on the home will be $3,780, and insurance will cost $535 a year. Other annual expenses will be: depreciation, $1,800; utilities, $2,400; maintenance, $1,600. Lost interest on their investment will be $975. Estimated income tax savings are $3,520. **a.** What are the total first-year costs of home ownership? **b.** What are the net costs in the first year of home ownership?

3. The Herndons bought a lot several years ago for $22,000. On the lot they own, they are now building a home that will cost $140,000. The Herndons will pay for the home by taking $25,000 from savings and borrowing the rest. First-year expenses are estimated to be: mortgage interest, $9,100; depreciation, 2.25% of the home's cost; property taxes, $2,890; insurance, $645; lost interest income, $720; maintenance, $1,350; utilities, $1,900. Income tax savings are estimated to be $3,025. **a.** What will be the Herndon's cost of owning the home in the first year? **b.** What will be the net cost of home ownership in the first year?

4. Alger and Stacy Walsh plan to buy the house they now rent. The monthly mortgage payment will be $1,228. They expect to pay $14,400 in annual interest and $3,600 a year in property taxes. Other first-year expenses are: depreciation, $2,660; insurance, $780; maintenance and repairs, $2,800; lost interest income, $585; utilities, $2,460. Estimated yearly tax savings are $5,040. What is the net cost of home ownership for the first year?

5. Timothy Lassauer leased an apartment for one year. The monthly rent is $900. Timothy's security deposit of one month's rent was returned to him at the end of the year, less $150 for carpet cleaning. Other annual costs of renting were: insurance on the apartment's contents, $110; utilities, $1,320. What was the total annual cost of leasing the apartment for one year?

Lesson 6.2 *Renting or Owning a Home*

6. Rita Zink and her two children live in subsidized housing and pay monthly rent of $230. The cost of heating is included in the rent. The electric bill averages $56 a month while the water and sewage bill averages $35 for every 3 months of use. Telephone costs average $19.50 a month. Rita carries no renters insurance on her personal property. What is Rita's total annual cost of renting?

7. Eunice Marshall lived in Key Cove Apartments for 12 months. She paid a monthly rent of $990 for her apartment and $35 a month to park in an attended lot. Her telephone expenses averaged $67 a month. The total annual cost of other utilities was $2,160; the cost of insurance was $155. Eunice received a refund of 50% of her one-month's security deposit at the end of her one-year lease. What total amount did Eunice spend on renting the apartment for a year?

8. The Mancini family rents a home for $1,150 a month plus $2,800 a year in related rental expenses. They could buy a similar home for $128,000, of which $20,000 represented the value of the lot. To make the down payment, they must withdraw $17,500 from a savings account that pays $1,120 annual interest. They estimate that their other first-year expenses would be: mortgage interest, $8,200; depreciation at 1.8% of the home's value; maintenance and repairs, $2,780; insurance, $480; property taxes, $3,050. The Mancini's estimate they would save $2,400 in income taxes by buying the home. **a.** What is the total net cost of home ownership? **b.** What total amount would be saved in the first year by buying a home instead of renting?

9. Cory Billingham is moving to another city. The cost of a one-bedroom apartment within a one-hour drive of the downtown area where he will work is $1,150 per month. The cost of utilities is expected to average $200 a month. Renters insurance would cost $175 a year. The least expensive home in good condition that Cory can find to buy costs $140,000. Annual expenses of owning the home will be property taxes, $3,240; mortgage interest, $11,520; depreciation, $2,800; maintenance and repairs, $2,600; insurance, $890; lost interest on investment, $350. Estimated income tax savings of home ownership are $4,000. Will it be less expensive for Cory to rent or to buy, and how much less?

Lesson 6.3 *Property Taxes*

Exercises

1. A school district is located in a city that has property with an assessed value of $105,600,000. The school budget for the coming year shows that $3,800,000 will be needed to operate the schools. Of this amount $450,200 will be received from state and federal governments.   **a.** What is the amount to be raised by taxes on local property owners?   **b.** What will be the tax rate, shown as a decimal rounded to three places?

2. Find the amount to be raised by property tax and the tax rate for each exercise. Show the tax rate as a decimal, correct to four places.

	Assessed Value	Total Expenses	Other Income	Raised by Property Tax	Tax Rate
a.	$31,050,000	$1,285,000	$113,100		
b.	$41,400,000	$1,140,000	$126,750		
c.	$26,162,000	$497,000	$88,920		
d.	$9,085,000	$514,900	$59,100		

3. Complete the chart below by changing the decimal tax rates to the equivalent rates shown.

	Decimal Rate	Dollars per $100	Dollars per $1,000	Cents per $1	Mills per $1
a.	0.046				
b.	0.0765				
c.	0.0084				
d.	0.04193				

Chapter 6 *Workbook*

Lesson 6.3 *Property Taxes*

4. The City of Ellenton's property tax rate is $5.238 on each $100 of assessed value. Arthur Winslow owns a home in Ellenton that is valued at $89,000 and is assessed at 50% of its value. **a.** What is the assessed value of Arthur's home? **b.** What is the property tax on Arthur's home?

5. Property worth $114,000 is assessed at 40% of its value. The property tax rate is $34.248 per $1,000 of assessed value. What is the tax on the property?

6. Danielle Lambert owns a home in the Village of Redson with a market value of $46,800. The assessed value of the home is $16,380. At Redson's property tax rate of 3.5¢ per $1 of assessed value, how much will Danielle pay in property taxes?

7. The property tax rate in New Guelph is 22.6 mills per dollar. What amount of tax is there on property assessed at $71,500?

8. In each exercise shown below, find the assessed value and the tax bill.

	Value of Property	Assessed Value		Tax Rate	Tax Bill
		Percent of Market Value	Amount		
a.	$80,000	80%		$3.875 per $100	
b.	$55,200	26%		$42.367 per $1,000	
c.	$138,000	50%		7.24 cents per $1	
d.	$32,100	100%		18.1 mills per $1	
e.	$195,100	35%		3.1 mills per $1	

Lesson 6.4 *Property Insurance*

Exercises

Round the annual insurance premiums to the nearest dollar for Exercises 1-11.

1. Rick Mueller insures his house for $88,500. **a.** Since the contents are automatically insured for 50% of the total insurance on the house, what is the amount the contents are insured for? **b.** If Rick's insurance company charges $0.53 per $100 for the policy, what will be the annual premium?

2. Amber Zahner's insurance company, the Rentin Group, charges $468 a year for $118,000 insurance coverage on her home. The Union Street Insurance Company quoted Amber a rate of $0.41 per $100 for the same coverage. **a.** What will be the annual premium for insurance from Union Street? **b.** By taking the less expensive policy, how much will Amber save a year?

3. Leon Schumacher insures his home for its full value of $68,000. The annual rate for the policy is $0.67 per $100. Increased coverage on the contents of the home will cost $45 more. Special coverage on a trading stamp collection will cost an additional $53. What is the total annual premium for all this coverage?

4. Delphia Loreno's home is insured for its value of $125,000, at a rate of $0.40 per $100. **a.** What is the total annual premium for this coverage? **b.** Her insurance company will deduct 2% from her annual premium if she installs smoke detectors or will deduct 6% if she installs a fire alarm system connected to the local fire station. If Delphia installs smoke detectors, how much annual premium will she pay? **c.** If a fire alarm system is installed instead, what would Delphia's annual premium be?

5. Frances Krusiewicz now pays $380 a year for $51,000 of home insurance with a $250 deductible. By choosing a $1,000 deductible policy she can save 30% of her annual premium. What will be the annual premium for the same policy with the higher deductible?

       Name ____ Date ___________

Lesson 6.4 *Property Insurance*

6. Scott Conlin rents an apartment and insures its contents with a renters policy. The value of the contents is $15,300, and the premium is $0.86 per $100. What is Scott's annual premium?

7. Annaliese Nuber insured the contents of her apartment for $22,500. The premium is $0.63 per $100 with a $750 deductible. Her personal property that is used away from home is insured at 10% of the policy's total coverage. Living expense coverage is 20% of the policy's total coverage. **a.** At what value is the personal property that she uses away from home insured? **b.** For what value is her living expense covered? **c.** What is the annual insurance premium that Annaliese pays?

8. A fire caused $1,810 damage to the Jackson family's kitchen. The Jackson's homeowner's insurance policy had a $250 deductible. Of the total damages, how much will the insurance company pay?

9. Ted Kotyla insured a rare book for its current value of $5,000 under a replacement cost policy. The book, which originally cost $2,600, was stolen from his home during a break in. The policy had a $100 deductible. What total amount would the insurance company pay for this loss?

10. A building valued at $150,000 is insured for $90,000 under an 80% coinsurance policy. A fire caused $14,000 damage. **a.** What was the face value of the policy? **b.** What was the required coinsurance amount? **c.** What amount of the loss did the insurance company pay?

11. A home valued at $400,000 is insured for $320,000 under a 90% coinsurance policy with a $500 deductible. The home had $4,100 of wind damage to its roof. **a.** What is the required coinsurance amount? **b.** What fractional part of the loss will the insurance company pay? **c.** What was the amount of damage paid by the insurer?

                                   Chapter 6 *Workbook*

Lesson 6.5 *Buying a Car*

Exercises

1. Bernadine Johnson plans to buy an Alaris four-door car with a MSRP of $21,040. The optional features Bernadine is considering and their suggested prices follow: alarm system, $415; larger tires, $84; accent stripes, $280; leather seats, $720; extended warranty, $625. At the car dealer's showroom she decides to add only the alarm system and extended warranty options to the basic Alaris car. What is the MSRP of the car and the options selected?

2. Nelson Valenti bought a car with an MSRP of $31,248. A 5% sales tax will be charged on the total purchase. Registration and license costs will be $110. Nelson plans to make a $3,000 down payment. **a.** What is the delivered price of the car? **b.** What is the balance due on this purchase?

3. The MSRP of a new van Lily McCarthy is buying is $28,752. State sales tax of 6.2% is charged on the purchase. The cost of license plates, title transfer, and other fees is $217. Lily will make a down payment of 10% of the van's MSRP. **a.** What is the delivered price of the van? **b.** What is the balance due on the transaction?

4. A two-year old car was placed on sale for $17,450. Herschel Cole made an offer to buy the car for $16,900, which the seller accepted. The sale of the car is subject to a 5.4% sales tax. Registration fees will be $45. New license plates will cost $87. What will be the delivered price of the car?

5. Bryce Gregory bought a four-year old car for $8,060 from a used car dealer. Bryce also purchased a one-year, 12,000 mile limited warranty for $250 through the dealer. Sales tax of 4% is charged on the purchase except for the warranty that is exempt from state sales tax. Bryce plans to make a down payment of 20% of the car's delivered price and take a loan for the balance. **a.** What is the delivered price of the used car? **b.** What is the balance due on the purchase?

Lesson 6.6 *Depreciating a Car*

Exercises

1. Noreen Tyson bought a new car for $19,560. She used the car three years and then traded it in for $10,200. **a.** What was the total depreciation for the three-year period? **b.** What was the average annual depreciation?

2. Zach Nieman bought a car 14 years ago for $13,308. He recently sold the car for $50 to a junkyard because the cost of repairing the engine was far greater than the car's value. **a.** What was the car's total depreciation? **b.** What was the average annual depreciation?

3. A wholesale company sold one of its trucks for $5,200. The truck cost $26,795 when it was bought seven years ago. **a.** What was the total depreciation on the truck for the seven-year period? **b.** What was the average annual depreciation?   **c.** What was the average annual rate of depreciation, rounded to the nearest tenth percent?

4. Nanette Dorow bought a four-wheel drive truck for $24,920. She used the truck for five years and then traded it in for $6,030. **a.** What was the average annual depreciation? **b.** What was the average annual rate of depreciation, rounded to the nearest tenth percent?

5. Spencer Frost estimates that his new car that cost $24,380 would be worth $13,500 after two years and $8,230 after five years. **a.** Based on Spencer's estimate, what will be the annual rate of depreciation, rounded to the nearest whole percent, for the first two years? **b.** What will the percent be for the five years?

   Chapter 6 *Workbook*

Name ____ Date __________

Lesson 6.7 *Car Insurance*

Exercises

Use the annual insurance table below to do Exercises 1 – 6.

Annual Insurance Premiums

Type of Insurance Coverage	Coverage Limits	Vehicle Used For		
		Pleasure Use Only	Driving to Work	Business
Bodily Injury	$25/$50,000	24.70	27.42	35.65
	$50/$100,000	37.06	41.14	53.48
	$100/$300,000	64.74	71.86	93.42
	$200/$500,000	82.54	91.62	119.11
Property Damage	$25,000	162.96	180.89	235.16
	$50,000	194.00	215.34	279.94
	$100,000	228.23	253.33	329.33
Collision	$100 deductible	559.84	621.42	807.85
	$250 deductible	478.12	530.71	689.92
	$500 deductible	422.34	468.80	609.44
Comprehensive	$100 deductible	150.38	166.92	216.00
	$250 deductible	128.64	142.79	185.63
	$500 deductible	105.38	116.98	152.07

1. Five cars are used as shown below. Each car is insured for bodily injury of $25/$50,000 and property damage of $25,000, unless noted otherwise. All have collision and comprehensive coverage with the deductibles shown. Find the annual premium for each type of coverage and the total annual premium.

	Car Usage and Deductibles	Annual Premium				
		Bodily Injury	Property Damage	Collision	Compre-hensive	Total
a.	For driving to work; collision, $250 deductible; comprehensive $100 deductible					
b.	For pleasure driving only; $100 deductible for both collision and comprehensive					
c.	For business; collision, $500 deductible; comprehensive, $100 deductible					
d.	For business; property damage, $100,000; $250 deductible for both collision and comprehensive					
e.	For pleasure driving only; collision $250 deductible; comprehensive, $250 deductible					

Lesson 6.7 *Car Insurance*

2. Rebecca Keyes owns an appliance repair company and uses her truck for business. She carries bodily injury coverage for $200/$500,000; property damage coverage for $50,000; collision, $100 deductible; comprehensive, $100 deductible. **a.** For this coverage, how much does she pay as an annual premium? **b.** If she chose a $500 deductible for both collision and comprehensive, how much would her annual premium be? **c.** By taking the higher deductibles how much would she save annually on truck insurance?

3. Before he retired, Eric Washburn drove his car to work and carried this insurance coverage: $25/$50,000 bodily injury, $50,000 property damage, $100 deductible for collision, and $250 deductible for comprehensive. **a.** For this coverage, how much did Eric pay as an annual premium? After he retired, Eric used his car only for pleasure driving and kept the same insurance coverage. **b.** How much does he pay for this coverage?

4. A truck used primarily for work on a farm is sometime used to deliver produce to markets. The truck is insured as being used for business. The truck is insured for the least amount of bodily injury and property damage insurance and for the highest deductibles for collision and comprehensive coverage. Because it is primarily a farm vehicle, a 15% discount is given off the regular annual premium. **a.** What is the premium before any discounts are given? **b.** What is the discount amount? **c.** What is the annual premium to be paid?

5. Blanche Isenhauer drives her car for pleasure and carries bodily injury coverage of $100/$300,000 and property damage coverage of $50,000. Her collision and comprehensive coverage is for the highest deductibles. **a.** At the rates found in the table, how much would the annual premium for this coverage be? As a young driver under the age of 25, however, Blanche is charged a total annual premium that is 1.8 times the total premium figured from the table. **b.** What is the annual premium that Blanche is charged?

6. Because he was convicted of drunk driving, Wilbert Garner may drive his car only to and from work. Wilbert's insurance company notified him that it will provide driving to work coverage, but at a rate 4 times the regular rate. Wilbert feels he can afford only the minimum coverage for bodily injury and property damage and the highest deductibles for collision and comprehensive coverage. For this insurance coverage, what annual premium will Wilbert pay?

Lesson 6.8   *Car Purchases and Leases*

Exercises

1. The delivered price of Leah St. Clair's new car is $22,450. She makes a $2,800 down payment and pays the balance in 36 monthly payments of $612. **a.** What total amount did Leah pay for the car? **b.** How much was the finance charge?

2. Being able to borrow money at a special interest rate of 3.3% was one of the reasons why Otto Kubik bought a new truck. The truck cost $19,865. Otto made a down payment of $1,865 and took a 48-month loan with payments of $405.76 monthly. **a.** What was the total amount Otto paid for the truck? **b.** How much did he pay in finance charges?

3. Suzanne Madigan leased a car for four years and drove the car 72,000 miles. Her monthly lease charge was $380.61. The leasing company charged $0.21 a mile for all miles driven over 60,000 miles. In addition, Suzanne had to pay a charge of $518.76 to repair a damaged door. **a.** Find the total of the monthly lease charges. **b.** What was the amount of the excess mileage charges? **c.** What was the total cost of leasing the car?

4. Foster Pruett leased a van on a 36-month contract at $418.53 per month. The lease terms allowed him 12,000 miles a year. Foster also purchased 7,500 extra, non-refundable miles at 9¢ a mile. In addition, he had to pay a $160 lease processing fee and a $750 down payment. Foster drove the van 40,162 miles in 36 months. **a.** What was the total of the monthly lease payments? **b.** What was the total cost of the extra miles purchase? **c.** What were Foster's total lease costs for the 36 months?

5. The 48-month lease terms on a truck that costs $20,650 are $340.11 monthly with a $650 down payment. The truck has an estimated residual value of $9,200. The truck may be purchased for a $2,780 down payment and 48 monthly payments of $448.93. **a.** What were the total costs of leasing? **b.** What were the total costs of buying? **c.** Is it more expensive to lease or buy the truck, and how much more expensive?

Lesson 6.8 *Car Purchases and Leases*

6. A SUV may be purchased for a delivered price of $27,340 with a 10% down payment and 36 monthly payments of $745.74. The vehicle may also be leased for $433.67 a month for 36 months. A down payment of $1,100 is required, and the SUV is assumed to be worth $14,200 at the end of the lease. **a.** Does leasing or buying the SUV cost more? **b.** How much more?

7. A 48-month lease plan on a luxury car that costs $46,700 consists of a $2,875 down payment, monthly payments of $594.80, and a residual value of $28,400. A purchase plan for the car requires a down payment of $3,250 and a 4-year loan with monthly payments of $1,082. **a.** What is the total cost of leasing? **b.** What is the total cost of purchasing? **c.** Which plan gives the lowest total cost? **d.** What is the difference in the plans over four years?

8. Marva Quinlan paid $17,980 cash as the delivered price for a truck. Her truck expenses for the first year were: gasoline, $988.56; insurance, $782.50; maintenance, $136.35; loss of interest on the truck's original cost, $719.20; and depreciation estimated at 26%. **a.** What was the total depreciation? **b.** What was the total truck operating expense for the year?

9. Orville Sewell leased a car for one year and drove it 21,854 miles. He spent $710 for insurance, $203.60 for maintenance, $1,420.51 for gas; $452 for a down payment, and $107 for registration and license fees. The leasing company charged $860 a month plus 19¢ a mile for each mile driven over 15,000 miles in a year. **a.** What was the total cost of operating the car for a year? **b.** What was the operating cost per mile, to the nearest cent?

10. Mary Jo Hurley paid $14,120 for a used car, including sales tax. During the first year she estimates the car's depreciation at 9.5% of the purchase price. Registration fees and license plates cost $112.50. Other costs were: insurance, $476; gas, $720; repairs and maintenance, $426; lost interest, $536.56. **a.** What was the total cost of operating the car for the first year? **b.** What was the operating cost per mile, to the nearest cent, if she drove 9,050 miles in the first year?

Term Puzzler

Directions Each group of scrambled letters can be sorted to spell a word or phrase. Unscramble the letters to form a word or phrase. Then sort the letters in boxes to form a key word.

a. Sort the scrambled letters below.

   1. terpoyp exsat

   2. gonicls stocs

   3. soicinlol

   4. rainceeditop

   5. eleas

   6. mipmuer

   7. tagomreg onla

   8. eelsar ualve

   9. tirecyus spedoit

  10. deervelid cepir

  11. teedbcludi

b. The key word is _____________________.

Chapter 6 *Workbook*

Integrated Project 6

Directions Read through the entire project before you begin doing any work.

Introduction Sonja and Quintin Stocker now rent an apartment for $820 a month. While renting, they saved $25,000 to use for a down payment on a house and car and pay for other purchasing costs. The Stockers have found a house priced at $156,000 that meets their needs. The local property tax assessment is 50% of a property's market value. Closing costs on the purchase of the house would be $3,150. Three lenders in their area offer mortgages at these terms:

Lender A requires a 15% down payment for a 7.25%, 20-year mortgage loan. For these terms, the monthly mortgage payment will be $1,048.

Lender B offers a 7.5%, 25-year mortgage loan with a minimum 10% down payment. The monthly mortgage payment will be $1,038.

Lender C offers the longest mortgage term, 30 years, at a rate of 7.875%. A minimum down payment of 5% is required. At these terms, the monthly mortgage payment will be $1,075.

The Stockers' combined gross income is $65,400 a year. If they buy the house, their property taxes will be $3.80 per $100 of assessed value. Other home expenses are: insurance, $518; maintenance and repairs, $1,700; lost interest on the down payment at 4% simple interest; depreciation at the rate of 2% a year on the value of the house, less the $38,000 value of the lot. The first-year mortgage interest they would pay to each lender is: Lender A, $9,513; Lender B. $10,462; Lender C, $11,625.

The Stockers will be able to itemize deductions on their income tax return because of the property taxes and mortgage interest they will pay when they buy the house. Depending on where they get their mortgage, their income tax benefits will be: Lender A, $1,996; Lender B, $2,282; Lender C, $2,334.

Because they will no longer live near where they work, the Stockers will need a second car that they want to buy instead of lease. The car they want sells for $18,140. To buy the car, they must make a 10% down payment and pay 7.74% interest. Their monthly payments would be $510 for a 3-year loan and $399 for a 4-year loan.

Estimated annual expenses of operating the second car are as follows: gasoline, 680 gallons at $1.55; insurance, $742; maintenance, $260; license fee, $61. Only one-half of the annual car insurance premium must be paid at the time the new car is purchased. The interest charges in the first year of the car loan would be $1,087 on a three-year loan and $1,136 on a four-year loan. If the car is purchased, the estimated depreciation expense the first year will be 25% of the purchase price. The interest lost on the down payment for the car will be $73.

Integrated Project 6, *continued*

Step One

Complete the following tables to summarize the data that the Stockers gathered.

Cash Needed for House and Car Purchases

(Assume minimum down payments are made)

	Lender A	Lender B	Lender C
Down Payment on House			
Closing Costs			
Subtotal			
Down Payment on Car			
Car Insurance (for one-half year)			
License Fee			
Total Amount Needed			

First-Year Cost of Owning House

Cost and Tax Savings Items	Mortgage Received From		
	Lender A	Lender B	Lender C
Property Taxes			
Insurance			
Maintenance and Repairs			
Lost Interest on Down Payment			
Depreciation			
Mortgage Interest			
Gross Cost of Owning			
Less Tax Savings			
Net Cost of Owning			

Mortgage Loan Analysis

	Lender A	Lender B	Lender C
Total Payments Over Term of Mortgage			
Mortgage Loan Amount			
Total Interest Paid Over Term of Mortgage			

Chapter 6 *Workbook*

Integrated Project 6, *continued*

First-Year Cost of Owning and Operating Second Car

	For 3-Year Loan	For 4-Year Loan
Gasoline		
Maintenance		
Insurance		
License Fee		
Depreciation		
Interest Lost on Down Payment		
Interest Paid on Car Loan		
Total Cost		

Total Payments for Mortgage and Car Loans for One Year

Mortgage Obtained from	Total Annual Mortgage Payment Plus Total Annual Car Loan Payment	
	3-Year Car Loan	4-Year Car Loan
Lender A		
Lender B		
Lender C		

Step Two

Answer the following questions.

1. In order to be approved for a mortgage loan by any lender, the loan amount must be less than 2.5 times the buyer's annual gross income. Do the Stockers meet this requirement? Why?

2. Do the Stockers have enough money in the bank to pay the down payments and other costs of buying the house and car and getting a loan for the house purchase from Lender A? from Lender B? from Lender C? Prove your answers.

3. If you were making this home and car buying decision for the Stockers, describe what you would do and why.

Name ____ Date ____________

Lesson 7.1 *Life Insurance*

Exercises

For all exercises in Exercises 1 – 4, use the life insurance annual premium table on page 283 in Chapter 7, Lesson , of the textbook. Treat all policyholders or customers as nonsmokers.

1. For each exercise, find the rate and annual premium for the amount of insurance, type of policy, and the type of customer indicated. Write each amount in the proper column in the form.

	Policy Type	Insured		Face of Policy	Rate from Table	Annual Premium
		Age	Gender			
a.	10-Yr.Term	25	Male	$100,000		
b.	Whole Life	45	Female	$250,000		
c.	10-Yr.Term	30	Female	$30,000		
d.	Whole Life	40	Male	$300,000		
e.	10-Yr.Term	20	Female	$15,000		

2. Reece Williams is 35 years old and bought a $175,000 term life insurance policy to insure that his daughter would have enough money to attend college in the event of his death. What is his annual premium?

3. Ned Viboda bought a $50,000 whole life insurance policy at age 20. What is his annual premium?

4. Gail Birnbaum just turned 30 and purchases a $350,000 term life insurance policy. What is her annual premium?

Name ____ Date ______________

Lesson 7.1 *Life Insurance*

5. Della Ahkta has a whole life policy for $50,000. She pays an annual premium rate of $13.47 per $1,000. When she signed her insurance contract she chose to use the annual dividend to reduce the annual premium. When she gets a notice that her insurance premium is due, she is notified that her policy has paid an annual dividend of $27.94. What amount will Della need to send the insurance company to pay the balance due on the annual premium?

6. Ryan O'Hara took out a whole life policy for $25,000 at the annual premium rate of $17.18 per $1,000. He paid premiums for 10 years. Over that time, the policy earned dividends totaling $254, and Ryan used them to reduce the premiums he paid. What was the total net premium payment to the insurance company over 10 years?

For Exercises 7 and 8, use the table of cash/loan values found on page 285 in Chapter 7, Lesson 1, of the textbook.

7. Tia Malverna took out a life insurance policy for $70,000. At the end of the fifteenth year, she turned in the policy for its cash value. How much did she receive from the insurance company?

8. When he took his first full-time job, Vittorio Rigazzi took out a whole life policy for $45,000. At the end of five years, Vittorio decided to cancel the policy for its cash value. What was the amount of money he received from the insurance company?

Name ____ Date ____________

Lesson 7.2 *Health Insurance*

Exercises

1. June Taylor's company pays 55% of her annual health insurance premium. If the total monthly premium for the insurance is $275, what is June's share of the annual premium?

2. As part of its benefits package, a company offers vision health insurance to employees. The monthly premium cost per employee is $43. If the employees pay 75% of the premium, how much is the total annual premium paid by an employee for the vision insurance?

3. Luis Santilla was hospitalized for an illness. The cost of his hospital room was $1,587. The cost of medical services was $1,298. His insurance company did not cover $359 of the total bill. Luis has to pay a $200 deductible and 20% coinsurance. What was the cost to Luis for treating his illness?

4. Olga Semargl's medical care bills for a recent illness were $4,620. Her major medical policy did not cover $312 of the bill. Olga's policy had a coinsurance feature that paid 80% of all covered expenses over a $500 deductible. **a.** What was the amount paid by the major medical policy? **b.** What was the total amount paid by Olga?

5. Ned Solon paid $145 per visit for 16 visits to a physical therapist to recover from an accident. His medical insurance policy paid 70% of the fees after subtracting Ned's deductible amount of $250. **a.** Of the total bill, how much did Ned pay? **b.** What amount did the insurance company pay?

Lesson 7.3 *Disability Insurance*

Exercises

1. Sheila Rodney works for a firm that provides a group disability policy for its employees with a benefit percentage of 58% of Sheila's average annual salary for the last 3 years. Her annual salary for the last 3 years was $25,800, $26,500, and $28,100. **a.** What is Sheila's average annual salary for the last 3 years? If Sheila were unable to work because of disability, what would be her monthly benefit amount?

2. Don Sevard's disability policy calculates his benefits percentage at 2.14% for each year he has worked for his company. If Don has worked for 20 years at the company, what is his benefits percentage?

3. Don Sevard's disability policy (see Exercise 2 above) will apply his benefit percentage to his average annual wages for the last 4 years. It will also reduce the benefits paid by the amounts Don receives from worker's compensation insurance. Don's wages for the last 4 years were $42,600; $45,100; $45,800, and $46,600.
   a. What was Don's average annual wage for the last 4 years? **b.** If he receives $345 monthly from worker's compensation, what will be his monthly income from his disability policy?

4. Tina Benald's group disability policy calculates the benefit percentage by adding 2% for each year that an employee works for the company. This benefit percentage is applied to an employee's average monthly compensation for the last 48 months. Tina worked for 15 years at the company at an average annual wage of $43,500 for the last 4 years. **a.** What is Tina's disability benefit percentage? **b.** What is Tina's average monthly salary for the last 4 years? **c.** What would Tina's monthly benefit amount be?

Lesson 7.4 *Buying Bonds*

Exercises

For Exercises 1 – 6, find the market price.

	Bond	Par Value	Quoted Price	Market Price
1.	Reliant Value	$1,000	102.874	
2.	Elison School District	$500	98.065	
3.	Demay Township Water Supply	$1,000	89.133	
4.	Korane Industries	$500	105.678	
5.	Tellor Assembly	$1,000	78.978	
6.	Velora Fabrics	$1,000	101.444	

7. Last year, Andy Bonner bought $1,000 par value Bemis Corporation bonds in these quantities and at these prices: 5 at 87.456; 10 at 107.379; 15 at 98.318. No commission was shown. Find Andy's total investment in Bemis bonds last year.

8. Marie Jagger buys eleven BuildMart $1,000 bonds at 92.347, plus $5.50 commission per bond. **a.** What is the market price of the eleven bonds? **b.** What is the total commission? **c.** What is Marie's total investment in the bonds?

9. Tony Delgado buys twenty $500 bonds at 104.812. The commission consists of a $20 transaction charge and a fee of $3 per bond. **a.** What is the market price of the twenty bonds? **b.** What is the commission? **c.** What is the total amount Tony invested in these bonds?

          Chapter 7 *Workbook*

Lesson 7.5 *Bond Interest*

Exercises

Find the total amount of quarterly or semiannual interest paid on the bonds below.

	No. Bonds	Par Value	Interest Rate	Interest Payments Made	Interest Amount Paid
1.	10	$1,000	7%	Quarterly	
2.	20	$500	8.50%	Semiannually	
3.	5	$1,000	6.25%	Quarterly	
4.	15	$1,000	9.40%	Semiannually	
5.	30	$500	11%	Quarterly	

6.   Alma Lasiter owns 25 Memphis Water 8.5%, $1,000 bonds. Find her annual income from the bonds?

Find the annual income and yield to the nearest tenth percent for each bond shown in the table.

	Par Value	Interest Rate	Annual Income	Quote	Market Price	Yield
7.	$500	8.00%		97.823	$489.12	
8.	$1,000	7.60%		105.473	$1,054.73	
9.	$1,000	12.00%		99.007	$990.07	
10.	$500	7.70%		101.789	$508.95	

11.   San-li Jen owns 50 Northern Railway System $1,000 bonds, paying $7\frac{1}{4}$% interest. San-li bought the bonds at 98.897. No commission was shown. Find the yield on each bond.

Lesson 7.5   *Bond Interest*

12. Murella O'Clancy buys a $500, 6.8% bond at 102.878, including the broker's commission. **a.** Find her annual income from the bond. **b.** Find her total investment in the bond.

13. Toulouse Armand buys 20 Padlack Company, $9\frac{1}{4}$%, $1,000 bonds at 96.782, plus $5 commission per bond. He also must pay $11.56 in accrued interest on each bond. Find his total investment in the bonds.

14. T. Barnes buys 10, $500, 8.5% bonds at 89.473. He pays $3.50 commission on each bond and $13.49 accrued interest on each bond. Find his total investment in the bonds.

15. R. Torre wants to earn an annual income of $2,375 from an investment in 9.5%, $1,000 bonds with a current market price of 101.563. **a.** To do so, how many bonds must he buy? **b.** How much must he invest?

Lesson 7.6 *Stocks*

Exercises

1. Find the total cost of each stock purchase below:

	No. of Shares	Name of Stock	Market Price	Commission	Total Cost
a.	100	Jeffries Shipping	$36.78	$87.15	
b.	200	Alliance Furniture	$101.85	$206.06	
c.	500	Creative Communications	$14.98	$194.55	
d.	300	Sandstone Pictures	$42.87	$247.33	
e.	400	Seiber Entertainment	$22.17	$201.15	

2. Marla Yeager placed an order with her broker for 300 shares of Barlow Chemical stock at $16.94. The broker bought the stock at that price and charged $146 commission. What was Marla's total investment in the stock?

3. Elton Johnson bought 500 shares of Alberta Steel stock at $46.12. On the purchase, the broker charged a commission of $79.60 for each 100 shares. What was the total investment that Elton made in Alberta Steel stock?

4. Tammy Roddick plans to buy 200 shares of ComTech stock at $15 a share. One broker's minimum commission charge on this purchase will be $100. A discount broker's minimum commission charge on this purchase will be $47. If Tammy uses the discount broker, what will be her total investment in this stock?

Lesson 7.6 *Stocks*

5. You invest in 200 shares of Lerner Windows stock and receive a semiannual dividend of $0.78 a share. At that rate, what will be your annual income from the investment?

6. Nadia Livuski owns 400 shares of Teton Materials stock, which has a par value of $79 a share. The stock pays a quarterly dividend of 1.8%. **a.** Each quarter, what is the amount of the dividend check that Nadia receives from the company? **b.** What is the annual income from the dividend checks?

7. Cedric McCarthy bought 800 shares of stock at a total cost of $28,096. The stock pays a semiannual dividend of $0.78 a share. **a.** What is the annual dividend income that Cedric receives? **b.** What yield, figured to the nearest tenth of a percent, does he earn on this investment?

8. Allegheny Lumber Company stock pays a quarterly dividend of 3% on its $35 par value. Laetika Vernier owns 400 shares of this stock that she bought at a total cost of $17,500. To the nearest tenth of a percent, what is the yield Laetika earns on her investment?

9. Intercomp Corporation stock pays a quarterly dividend of $0.21 a share. Albert Zagreb buys 600 shares of the stock at $26, and pays $308 commission. **a.** How much did Albert invest? **b.** On his investment, how much does Albert receives as annual income? **c.** What is the yield to the nearest tenth of a percent.

Chapter 7 *Workbook*

Lesson 7.6 *Stocks*

10. Leland Corelli sold 200 shares of DataFeed Company at $53.78. His broker charged a commission of $219.50. Other selling charges amounted to $2.16. From this sale, how much net proceeds did Leland receive?

11. Wanda Dirkson sold 200 shares of the 500 shares that she holds of Banff Corporation. She sold the shares at $9.77 and paid a total charge of $75.98 for commission and other selling expenses. **a.** How much net proceeds did Wanda receive from this sale? **b.** Based on the selling price she got for the 200 shares, how much are the remaining shares that Wanda owns worth?

12. Mike Lymann bought 200 shares of Basset Exploration Company on Monday at a total cost of $7,685. He sold all the shares a month later at 45.28 and paid a commission of $179.50. What was the amount of profit or loss from this sale?

13. Tanya Wilson bought 500 shares of stock at a total cost of $15,630. She received two quarterly dividends of $0.45 per share and then sold the stock, receiving net proceeds of $16,038. **a.** What were the total dividends she received? **b.** What was her profit from the sale of the stock? **c.** What was her total gain from owning and selling the stock?

14. Karl Schmidt bought 300 shares of stock at a total cost of $6,924. He kept the stock for three years. During this time, he received semiannual dividends of $1.38 per share. He then sold the stock and received net proceeds of $6,287. **a.** What were the total dividends he received? **b.** What was his loss on the sale of the stock? **c.** What was his net gain from owning and selling the stock?

Lesson 7.7 *Mutual Funds*

Exercises

Use the information in the following mutual fund quotation tables to solve all the exercises in this lesson.

Fund Name	NAV	Offer Price
Avion Balanced	21.56	22.34
Bueter Growth	11.54	N.L.
Carter Income	15.60	16.51
Delmar High Yield	8.45	8.89
Eagle Health	5.89	N.L.

Fund Name	NAV	Offer Price
Farley International	25.78	N.L.
Gardner Technology	32.76	N.L.
Harris Large Cap	29.88	32.13
Isaacs Transportation	14.06	15.02
Jubal Green	16.55	N.L.

1. Find the total investment in each mutual fund.

	Fund Name	Shares Purchased	Total Investment
a.	Avion Balanced	500	
b.	Bueter Growth	200	
c.	Carter Income	100	
d.	Delmar High Yield	1,000	
e.	Eagle Health	400	

2. Find the number of shares purchased to the nearest thousandth share.

	Fund Name	Total Investment	Shares Purchased
a.	Farley International	$5,000	
b.	Gardner Technology	$1,000	
c.	Harris Large Cap	$7,500	
d.	Isaacs Transportation	$4,300	
e.	Jubal Green	$10,000	

     Chapter 7 *Workbook*

Lesson 7.7 *Mutual Funds*

Exercises

3. Find the commission rate charged on purchases of these load funds, correct to the nearest tenth.

	Fund Name	Commission Rate
a.	Avion Balanced	
b.	Bueter Growth	
c.	Carter Income	
d.	Delmar High Yield	
e.	Eagle Health	

4. An investor bought 1,000 shares of Eagle Health mutual fund at the price quoted in the mutual fund tables. She then sold the shares a year later for $6.82 a share. **a.** What was the total investment the investor made in Eagle Health? **b.** What were the total proceeds the investor received from the sale of the Eagle Health shares? **c.** What was the profit or loss the investor made on the investment?

5. a. What was Matayka Robin's total cost of buying 100 shares of Carter Income fund at the price quoted in the mutual fund tables? **b.** If she sells all the shares she owns at $16.25, what are her proceeds from the sale? **c.** What will be the profit or loss from the investment?

6. Paul Zorbina bought $10,000 worth of Harris Large Cap mutual fund shares at the offer price quoted in the mutual fund tables. He then sold the shares two years later for $38.78 a share. **a.** What was the total number of shares Paul bought, to the nearest thousandth share? **b.** What was the total commission that he paid when he bought the shares? **c.** What were the proceeds Paul received from the sale of the shares? **d.** What was the profit or loss Paul made on the investment?

Lesson 7.8 *Real Estate*

Exercises

1. Tarn Yesrak bought a resort cottage. He used a rental property company to manage maintenance and rentals. The company charged him $100 per month for maintenance and 25% of the rental income. Last year, the condominium was rented for 30 weeks at $1,000 a week. For last year, he paid $11,850 in mortgage interest and $3,260 for taxes, insurance, and other expenses. **a.** What was his gross income? **b.** What were his total expenses? **c.** What was his net income?

2. Tanya Jackson bought a house and during the first year, was able to rent it for only 7 months at $620 a month. Though the house was vacant for 5 months, Tanya had to pay average expenses of $175 a month for the whole year. She also paid $3,600 in mortgage interest. **a.** For the first year, what was Tanya's gross income? **b.** What was her net income or net loss?

3. Jim Lin made a down payment of $36,000 in cash for a two-unit apartment. In the first year, he rented one unit for 12 months, the other for 8 months. The monthly rental of each unit was $740. Jim's expenses for the year were: mortgage interest, $3,980; taxes, $1,660; insurance, $1,120; repairs, $1,000; depreciation at 3% of the property value of $142,000. **a.** For the year, what was Jim's earned gross income? **b.** What were his total expenses? **c.** What was his net income?

4. Using the information in Exercise 3, find Jim's rate of income on his cash investment, figured to the nearest tenth percent.

5. Last year Sally O'Malley bought an apartment house that brought in $6,900 a month in rental income. The building cost her $420,000. Sally paid $150,000 in cash for it and gave a mortgage for the rest. She paid $35,220 in mortgage interest, and other expenses, including depreciation, were $22,080 year. **a.** What was Sally's net income? **b.** This is equivalent to what rate of income on her cash investment?

Chapter 7 *Workbook*

Lesson 7.8 *Real Estate*

Exercises

6. For each exercise, find the annual and monthly rent needing to be charged.

	Type of Rental Property	Value	Owner's Cash Investment	Annual Net Income Wanted	Annual Expenses	Annual Rent Needed	Monthly Rent Needed
a.	Office Suite	$180,000	$27,000	12%	$25,300		
b.	Warehouse	$256,000	$51,200	15%	$24,320		
c.	Store	$146,000	$14,600	14%	$16,380		
d.	Apartment Building	$450,000	$90,000	13%	$67,500		
e.	Lake Cabin	$225,000	$56,250	8%	$24,300		

7. Ira Friedman made a $68,000 down payment on an apartment worth $ 362,000. His total mortgage interest for the first year was $34,120, and other expenses totaled $15,600. In the first year, he spent $9,800 for a new porch and entranceway and $6,400 for a security system. At the end of the first year, what was Roy's total capital investment in the apartment building?

8. Ina Dreyfus plans to buy a cabin worth $32,000 by making an $8,000 down payment. She estimates that her yearly expenses of owning the cabin will be $6,280. Ina also estimates that she will be able to rent the cabin for only seven months a year. What is the monthly rent, to the nearest whole dollar, that Ina must charge if she wants to earn 8.5% on her investment?

9. Robert Taylor made a $16,000 down payment on a home worth $130,000. To make the home accessible for all potential renters, he paid $4,250 to install ramps and handrails at the front and rear entrances. Wall repairs and painting cost $1,750 and another $1,250 was spent to replace defective wiring. What was Robert's capital investment in the home?

Name ____ Date ____________

Lesson 7.9 *Retirement Investments*

Exercises

1. Ali Zahir is retiring at age 65. He will receive the following monthly amounts: $1,200 from his union pension and $984 from social security. He will also draw $500 a month from a private pension fund he owns. What will be his total annual retirement income?

2. Molly Feldman is 66 and receives $911 in monthly pension from her company and $675 monthly from social security. She wants her monthly retirement income to be $2,500 a month. What percent of her $350,000 IRA must Molly withdraw each month to reach the monthly income she wants, to the nearest tenth percent?

3. Troy White is 67 and his monthly retirement income is made up of $1,500 from his employer-based pension fund and $890 from social security. He also has an IRA worth $250,000. What percent of his IRA nust Troy withdraw each year if he wants his total retirement income to be $38,400 a year?

4. Gina Lopata paid in $64,000 to her pension fund during the 25 years she worked for her company. Gina's fund pays $6.50 a month for each $100 of pension funds contributed if she retires at age 65. What will be the amount of her monthly pension at age 65?

5. John Markum's pension fund pays 2.3% of his average salary for the last three years for each year that he contributes to the fund. His annual salary for the last three years was $47,800, $48,500, and $49,800. John has contributed to his pension fund for 25 years. **a.** What was John's average salary for the last three years? **b.** What is John's total pension rate? **c.** If John retires now, what will his monthly pension amount be?

     Chapter 7 *Workbook*

Lesson 7.9 *Retirement Investments*

6. Magda Rohas has worked for Telley, Inc. for 29 years. She was paid $3,200 a month two years ago, $3,500 a month last year, and is paid $3,900 a month this year. Magda's pension fund pays a benefit rate of 2.25% for each year of service to the company and applies this to her average salary for the last three years before retirement. **a.** If Magda retires at the end of this year, what will be her average monthly salary for the last three years? **b.** What will Magda's total pension rate be? **c.** What is the monthly pension amount that Magda will receive?

7. Zuba Nazeer is 78 years old and has an IRA totaling $508,150. What is the amount she must withdraw, as a minimum, from her IRA this year?

8. Ty O'Hara's IRA total is $491,200. What is the minimum amount he must withdraw from his IRA this year, if he is 73?

9. Tien Kuo celebrated her eighty-fourth birthday on January 3. She has a total investment in her IRA of $617,800. What is the minimum amount she must withdraw from the investment this year?

10. Wally Brennan works for a state college. Wally's state pension fund reduces the total pension rate he will receive by $\frac{1}{2}$% for each year that he retires before the age of 65. If Wally retires at age 58, by what percent will his pension be reduced?

11. Mehta Olgilvie withdrew $5,435 from her IRA when she was 53. What was the amount of penalty she paid?

12. Subina Kruegg took out $10,500 from her IRA when she was 58. **a.** What penalty did she pay on the withdrawal? **b.** What is the net amount she received?

Term Puzzler

Directions Some of the terms listed below are in the puzzle. Circle each term when you find it. It may be written downward, upward, sideways, or diagonally. There are 15 terms in the puzzle. How many can you find?

beneficiary

bond discount

bond premium

bonds

capital investment

cash value

coinsurance

disability insurance

group health insurance

health insurance

IRA

life insurance

major medical insurance

market price

mutual fund

net asset value

offering price

par value

policy

term life insurance

worker's compensation

yield

```
D I S A B I L I T Y I N S U R A N C E N K
P N Q L Q H E A L T H I N S U R A N C E K
B O N D D I S C O U N T I S Y S D R N G L
O O F F E R I N G P R I C E H B I G L H G
N Y N C C A P I T A L I N V E S T M E N T
D E K D K M H O L B B H A W H T V A M M Y
P E V L S I N S I P J L H H Q M L T E Y R
R P Y J V K A Y W Z U H J I Y T D U C L V
E L B J N E W E L E W U L L L O F M A R X
M A J O R M E D I C A L I N S U R A N C E
I A B N J Y V S J K M E D G C L I P R D U
U X R C G H H U V I R I K M X M L O U N L
M J X K N E T A S S E T V A L U E P S H Y
R S V Q E W S I B P D T G Q I T I E N H J
P G J L N T F R D B J L L N V U G M I G K
A G V C M M P P C O I N S U R A N C E Q O
D J T J Q E P R G X V Z Y I C L H N F U M
U U M E S Q O I I N J Z J P D F E V I H U
D G S F L J O E E C N I J F P U Q A L T O
W Y D F E Z Q X J N E B E P G N X R U J M
K R W Q F V C E F D O I I G B D O U T Y M
```

Integrated Project 7

Directions Read through the entire project before you begin doing any work.

Ramon Palonco is 35 years old and works in the accounting department for BiState Materials, Inc. His wife, Alicia Cabria-Palonco, is a mathematics teacher in a nearby high school. Alicia's mother, Carmen, is also a teacher. Carmen has taught elementary school for 40 years in the same school district as her daughter.

Step One
Ramon decides to buy a whole life policy in the amount of $150,000.

1. Using the premium table on page 283 of the textbook, his annual premium is _________.

2. Using the cash value table on page 285 of the textbook, the policy's cash value will be _________ when he is 55.

Step Two
Alicia was recently hospitalized for a serious illness. The total bill for her medical care was $12,780. Alicia's medical insurance only covered $11,960 of the bill. The insurance company also subtracted a $500 deductible and her policy requires her to pay 15% in coinsurance.

3. The insurance company paid _________ of the hospital bill.

4. Alicia had to pay _______ of the total bill.

Step Three
Ramon's group disability policy pays 2.2% for each of the 15 years that he has worked for the company as a benefit percentage. The benefit percentage is applied to the average of his salary for the last three years. Ramon earned $42,500, $44,200, and $46,300 as salaries in his last three years.

5. Ramon's benefit percentage is ______%.

6. Ramon would receive ___________ each month from his policy if he were totally disabled at this time.

Integrated Project 7, continued

Step Four

Alicia and Ramon bought 10, $1,000 bonds at 95.363. Their broker charged them $3.50 per bond as commission.

7. The market price of each bond was ___________.

8. Their total investment in the bonds was ___________.

Step Five

Alicia and Ramon decide to sell 200 shares of Norma Drilling Company stock at $24.16. Their broker's commission and other charges were $126.15.

9. The net proceeds from the sale of the stock were ______________.

Step Six

Alicia and Ramon use the net proceeds from the sale of their stock to purchase 150 shares of Madison Energy Funds, a mutual fund with a NAV of 29.20 and an offering price of 30.66.

10. The total investment the couple made in the mutual fund was ___________.

11. The rate of commission their broker charged them, to the nearest tenth percent, was _____%.

Step Seven

Alicia's mother, Carmen, has decided to retire this year after 40 years of teaching. Her pension fund pays 1.95% of her average salary for the last four years for each year of service to the school district. Carmen's salary for the last four years was $48,300, $50,200, $51,700, and $53,300.

12. Carmen's annual retirement pension will be ________________.

13. Carmen's monthly pension amount will be ________________.

Lesson 8.1 *Measures of Central Tendency*

Exercises

1. Sort each group of numbers into ascending order. Then find the mean, median, mode, and range of each group.

Number Group	**Mean**	**Median**	**Mode**	**Range**
a. 6, 8, 22, 7, 3, 4, 16, 6				
b. 34, 56, 53, 42, 46, 48, 34, 40, 34				
c. 5.6, 5.4, 6.2, 6.0, 6.8, 5.4, 6.1, 5.7				

2. The daily number of job applicants at a factory during one month follow: 12, 7, 9, 14, 8, 7, 9, 11, 13, 12, 9, 10, 12, 14, 15, 9, 9, 12, 15, 9, 10, 8, 11, 12, 15, 11, 14. Use the form below to complete a frequency distribution table for the factory. For the number of applicants: **a.** What is the mean? **b.** What is the median? **c.** What is the mode?

Number of Applicants *Frequency Distribution Table*		
Item	**Frequency**	**Total**
7	// 2	14
8	//	
9	////// /	
10	//	
11	///	
12	/////	
13	/	
14	///	
15	///	

Lesson 8.2 *Probability*

Exercises

1. A box contains six disks that are the same size. Four are red and numbered 1, 2, 3, and 4. Two are blue and numbered 5 and 6. Pick one disk from the box of disks. What is the probability of each of event?

   a. Picking a red disk.

   b. Picking a disk with a number less than 7.

   c. Picking a green disk.

   d. Picking a disk with a number greater than 6.

   e. Not picking a red disk.

   f. Picking a disk marked with an odd number.

   g. Picking a disk marked 4.

   h. Picking a disk with a number not greater than 2.

   i. Picking a disk not marked 2.

   j. Picking a disk numbered either 1 or 6.

2. A carmaker found 7 defective door latches out of 350 vehicles specifically inspected for this defect. **a.** What is the percent of vehicles with defective latches? **b.** How many vehicles with defective latches could the carmaker expect to find out of the 146,000 vehicles already sold?

3. The quality inspectors rejected 3 hand mixers due to imperfections in the case out of 1,250 mixers inspected. **a.** This represented a defect rate of what percent? **b.** Based on this defect rate, how many mixers out of an annual production of 225,000 mixers would be rejected because of case defects?

4. Use the mortality table to find the probability, to the nearest hundredth, of each person living to the projected age.

Name	Present Age	Projected Age	Probability of Reaching Projected Age
a. V. Carr	Born today	60	
b. X. Castro	40	50	
c. T. Barry	10	70	
d. M. Wolfe	30	80	
e. C. Hansen	20	40	

Mortality Table	
Age	**Number Living**
0	100,000
10	97,000
20	96,000
30	95,000
40	93,000
50	90,000
60	82,000
70	66,000
80	39,000

Name ____ Date ____________

Lesson 8.3 *Bar and Line Graphs*

Exercises

1. The vertical bar graph below shows the sales of Wilkin's Tile for each quarter of last year. At the right of the graph, write the dollar volume of sales shown by each bar figure on the vertical bar graph below.

2. The monthly sales of Eagle Pottery Works for the first four months of the year are: January, $24,000; February, $28,000; March, $25,000; April, $36,000. Show these sales figures on the vertical bar graph below.

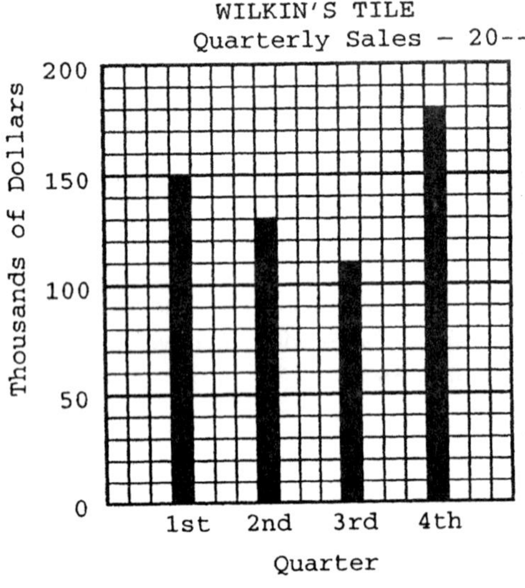

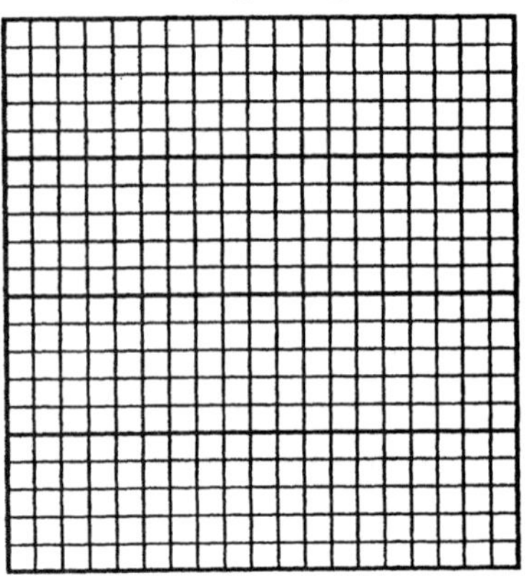

3. The horizontal bar graph below shows the sales made by six salespersons for the week ending August 8. At the right of the graph you are to write the amount of each salesperson's sales.

4. The sales of Cruz Greenhouses for April were shrubs, $35,000; sod, $28,000; trees, $12,000; fertilizer, $24,000; garden tools, $17,000. Show these facts on the horizontal bar graph.

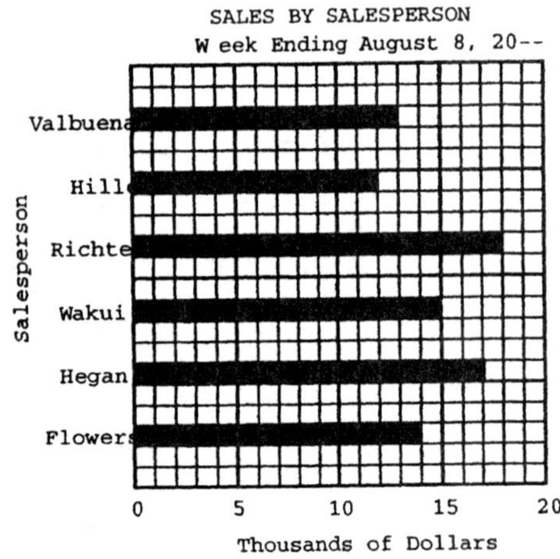

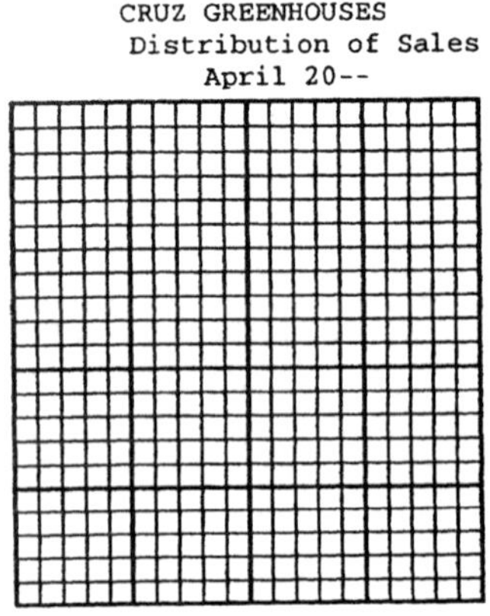

Lesson 8.3 *Bar and Line Graphs*

5. The number of cruise information packets mailed by the Bailey Travel Agency last year were these:

January	100	May	170	September	180
February	120	June	240	October	200
March	160	July	320	November	260
April	200	August	230	December	360

Use the graph paper at the right to show these facts in a vertical bar graph.

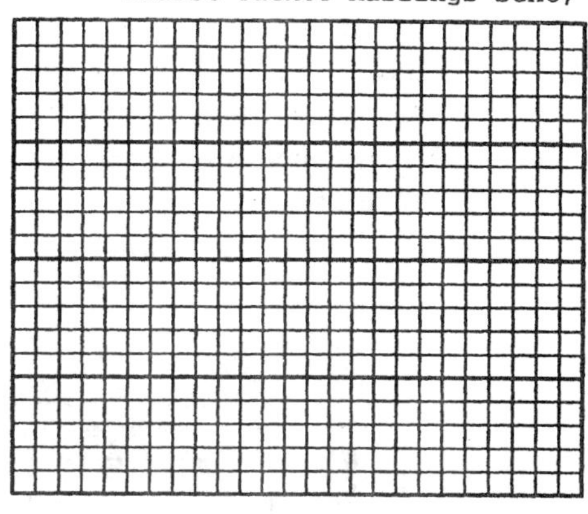

6. The line graph below shows Tobin Craft Company's monthly sales for last year and this year. Answer these questions about the graph. **a.** In what month were this year's sales the smallest? **b.** In what month were sales this year the greatest? **c.** For March, what were last year's sales and this year's sales? **d.** Sales were lower this year than last year in which months? **e.** The greatest difference between sales of the two years was in what month? **f.** What was the difference?

7. Li-ming Su's commission income for the first ten weeks of last year and this year are shown below.

Week	Last Year	This Year
1	350	370
2	370	400
3	400	340
4	480	390
5	520	450
6	550	530
7	530	580
8	500	520
9	490	470
10	460	430

From these figures, make a line graph showing the income for this year, using a solid line; and the income for last year, using a dashed line.

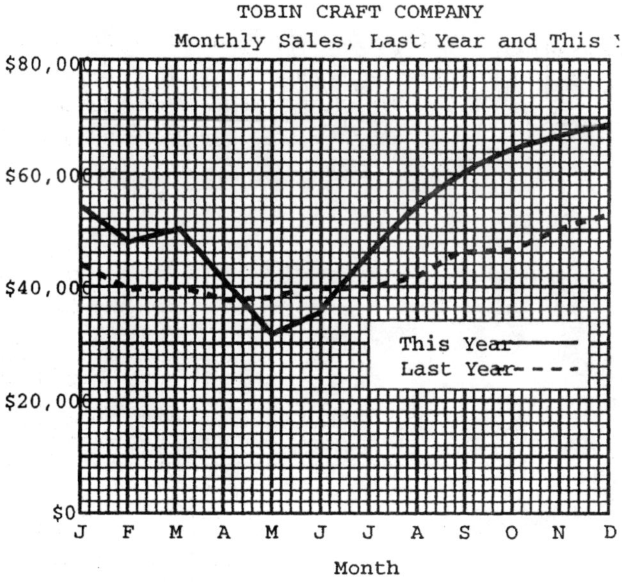

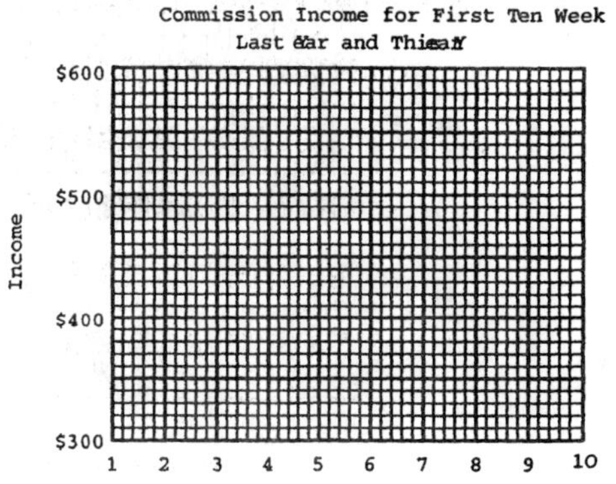

Lesson 8.4　*Circle and Rectangle Graphs*

Exercises

1. The owner of Chef's Choice Cutlery wants to show the type of sales for last year by making the rectangle graph below. The total sales for last year were $620,000. You are to write in the blank spaces on the graph the amount of the **a.** Internet sales;　**b.** fax/mail order sales; **c.** home demonstration sales; **d.** in-store sales.

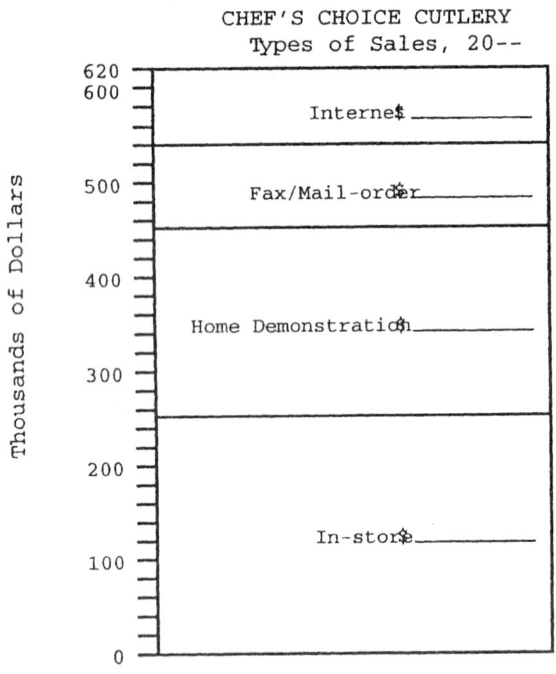

3. While on a business trip, Ida Koval spent $1,680. Ida wants to make a circle graph comparing the different expenses of her trip. The sections of the graph are based on these figures taken from her expense record: lodging, $588; meals with customers, $504; samples, $420; car, $134.40; other, $33.60. You are to find the percent each item is of the total expenses. Show these percents in the circle graph below.

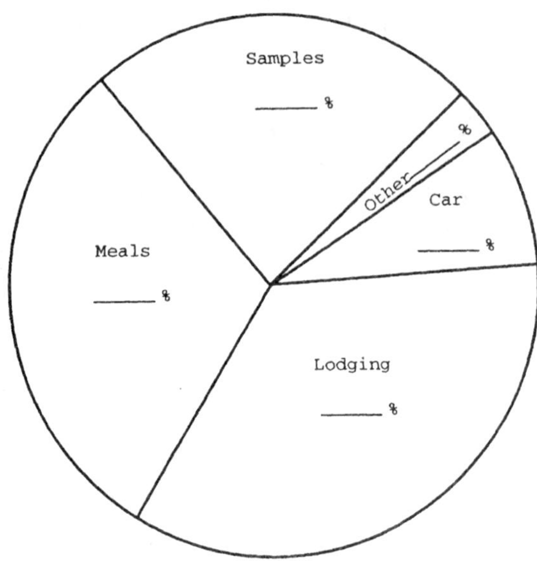

2. These amounts were spent last year by the Chandler Employment Agency to update their offices: equipment, $16,000; furniture, $10,000; carpeting, $8,000; security system, $6,000. Use the form at the right to make a horizontal rectangle graph showing those amounts as percents of the total upgrade expense.

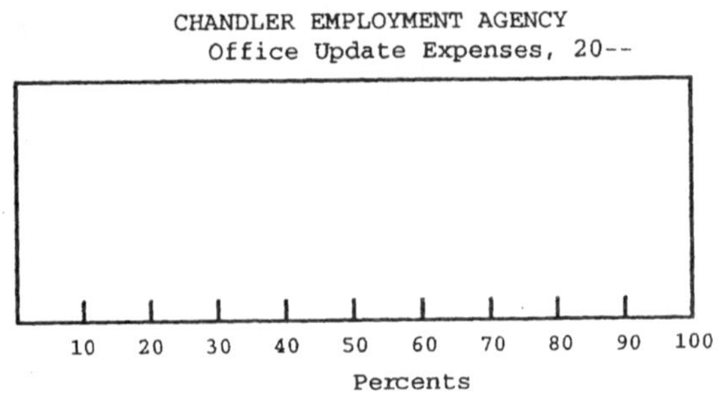

Lesson 8.4 *Circle and Rectangle Graphs*

4. The owner of Tina's Book Bargains estimates that her shop's total annual sales come from these items, stated as percents: fiction books, 45%; nonfiction books, 30%; reference books, 20%; magazines, 5%. Show the items on the circle graph below. Label each part of the circle graph.

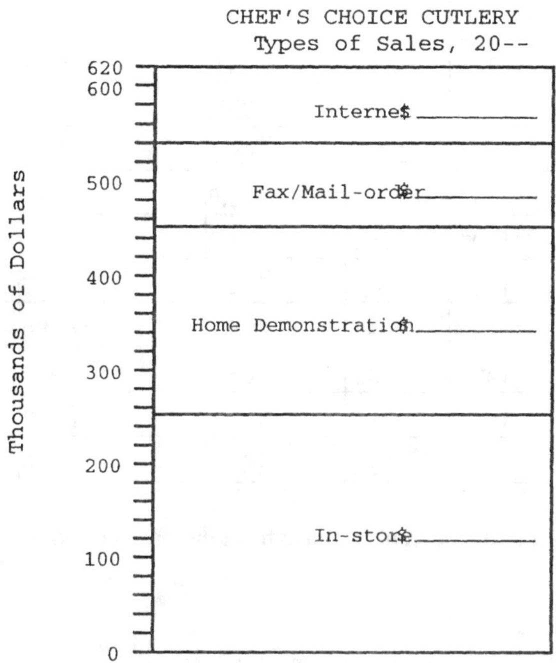

5. The Spaulding Cleaning Company estimates that its $800,000 in revenue last year came from cleaning the interiors of buildings owned by these customers: retail stores, 25%; insurance companies, 40%; city government, 20%; community college, 15%; Figure the amount of revenue earned from each customer and show those amounts on the horizontal rectangle graph below.

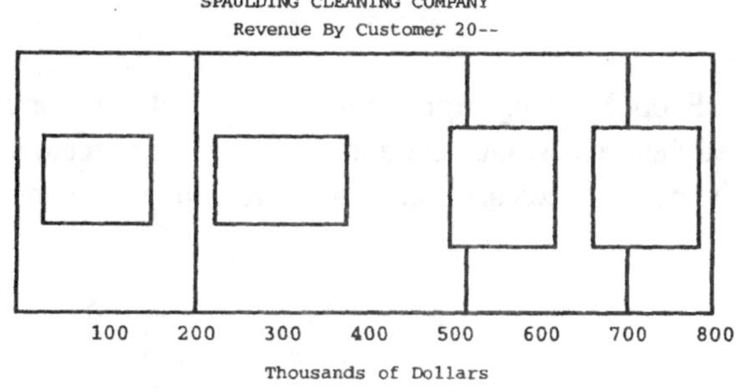

6. The Auto Stop's total sales last year came from installing these items in cars: sound systems, $150,000; alarms, $100,000; sun roofs, $200,000; phones, $50,000.

a. What were the total sales last year?

What is the percent each item represents of the total sales?

b. stereo systems

c. alarms

d. sunroofs

e. phones

Show these percents on the rectangle graph below.

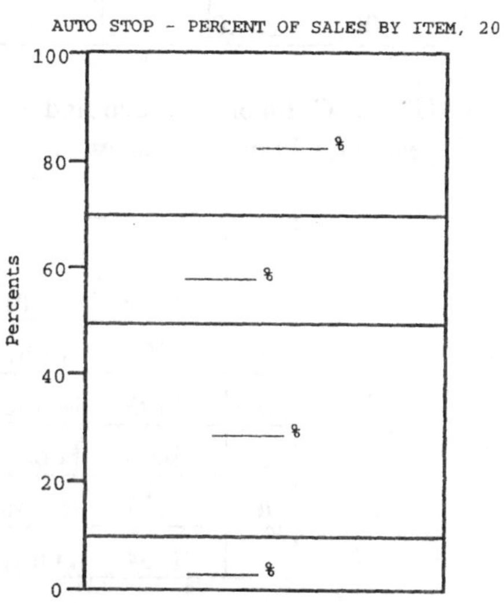

Lesson 8.5 *Economic Statistics*

Exercises

Historical Report -- Consumer Price Index, 1990-1999									
Categories of Goods and Services									
Years	**All Items**	**Food**	**Housing**	**Apparel**	**Transport ation**	**Medical Care**	**Recreation**	**Education and Communication**	**Other**
1982-84	100.0	100.0	100.0	100.0	100.0	100.0	---	---	100.0
1994	148.2	147.2	145.4	130.5	137.1	215.3	93.0	90.3	202.4
1995	152.4	150.3	149.7	130.6	139.1	223.8	95.6	93.9	211.1
1996	156.9	156.6	154.0	130.3	145.2	230.6	98.5	97.1	218.7
1997	160.5	159.1	157.7	131.6	143.2	237.1	100.0	100.0	230.1
1998	163.0	162.7	161.3	130.7	140.7	245.2	101.2	100.7	250.3
1999	166.6	165.9	164.8	130.1	148.3	254.2	102.0	102.3	263.0
2000	172.2	170.5	171.9	127.8	154.4	264.8	103.7	103.6	274.0
2001	177.1	175.3	177.6	124.8	149.0	278.3	105.3	106.9	287.0
2002	179.9	177.8	181.1	121.5	154.2	291.3	106.5	109.2	295.8
2003	184.0	184.1	185.1	119.0	154.7	302.1	107.7	110.9	300.2

1. Use the CPI table above to find the index number and the percent increase from the base period for each year and CPI category shown below.

	Year	**CPI Category**	**Index Number**	**Percent Increase From Base Period**
a.	2000	All Items		
b.	1995	Medical Care		
c.	2003	Food		
d.	1997	Housing		
e.	1994	Transportation		

2. Use the CPI table and compare the categories of Food, Housing, Apparel, and Transportation for 1996 with the base period. Which category: **a.** showed the greatest increase and what was the percent increase? **b.** showed the smallest increase and what was the percent increase? **c.** had a percent increase nearest to the increase for the "All Items" category?

Lesson 8.5 *Economic Statistics*

3. Use the CPI table to find the rate of inflation for these years, to the nearest tenth percent: **a.** 1997? **b.** 1999? **c.** 2001?

4. Of the categories Housing and Transportation: **a.** Which had the higher rate of inflation between 1994 and 2000, to the nearest percent? **b.** What was the higher rate?

5. What was the rate of inflation, to the nearest tenth percent, for Education and Communication: **a.** in 1995; **b.** in 1999?

6. For the Recreation category, find the rate of inflation, to the nearest tenth percent, for: **a.** 1994; **b.** 1997.

7. **a.** What was the Food category index number in the CPI in 2003? **b.** Compared to the base period, by 2003 the cost of food had increased by what percent? Assume that the price of a box of cereal costing $1.70 in the base period increased at the same rate as all food prices. **c.** What would have been the price of cereal in 2003, to the nearest cent?

8. Use the CPI table to calculate the purchasing power of the dollar for these years, to the nearest tenth of a cent: **a.** 1999; **b.** 2002; **c.** 1996; **d.** 2000

9. A report states that the unemployment rate for all persons in the labor force increased to 7.4% from 6.8% six months ago. **a.** For every 100,000 persons in the labor force, what number are now unemployed? **b.** How many more persons per 100,000 are now unemployed than 6 months ago?

10. The unemployment rate among the 140,000 persons in the labor force in Buell County is 8.4%. **a.** What is the number of persons who are unemployed? **b.** What is the number of persons who are employed?

Term Puzzler

Complete the crossword puzzle below. Some answers are two words placed together without space between them.

Across

1. Samples selected from a group by chance
3. An event that is the outcome of making a random choice
6. The middle number in a group
7. Rise in the prices of goods and services
9. Sum of numbers divided by number of items
10. Rate showing percent of labor force not working
11. Past time period with which comparisons are made
13. 100% of this graph is 360°
14. Table showing people living to certain age
15. A way of predicting the outcome of an event

Down

1. A graph that may be shown vertically or horizontally
2. The number that appears most frequently in a group
4. Graph having bars drawn from left to right
5. Difference between highest and lowest number in a group
8. Type of distribution table that shows data in order
12. A graph where bars are drawn up and down

Integrated Project 8

Directions Read through the entire project before you begin doing any work.

Introduction The Pro-Image Company produces special-order, logo sweatshirts for sale to resorts, ski lodges, golf courses, schools and universities, community agencies, and other organizations. It also sells a private-brand of shirts to the general public through its Internet website. The owner of the Pro-Image Company will soon meet with the company's manager to review production, sales, and other financial data. As an assistant to the manager, one of your jobs is to keep statistical records and to help prepare reports.

For the meeting, you are to prepare a graph of the Pro-Image Company's operations that shows the company's third quarter operating results, which are now available. Statistics on employee absences and their cost to the business must also be calculated. In addition, the effect on company costs of pay increases due employees must be calculated.

Customer orders usually arrive from three weeks to four months before the custom apparel is produced and shipped. "Unit sales" are recorded when the products are shipped to customers. "Unit production" is recorded as the products are produced.

Step One

Unit production and sales figures for the first three quarters of the year are shown in the worksheet below. Round the actual production and sales figures to the nearest 2,500 units and enter the results in the "rounded" column.

Pro-Image Company
Quarterly Production and Sales Summary

Month	Unit Production		Unit Sales	
	Actual	**Rounded**	**Actual**	**Rounded**
January	65,095		61,070	
February	70,010		66,310	
March	77,590		64,750	
April	106,122		80,900	
May	88,965		103,862	
June	96,218		99,078	
July	96,912		102,786	
August	99,874		109,680	
September	88,901		86,012	

Integrated Project 8, continued

Step Two

Use the graph paper below to make a line graph showing the Pro-Image Company's unit production and unit sales data for the first three quarters of the year. The graph paper has five blocks to the inch. Follow these steps:

1.   Label the graph with the company's name and the title of the graph.

2.   Begin at the left of the horizontal scale and leave the first two blocks empty. Then make a mark for January and mark off every fourth block for the remaining months. Write abbreviations for the names of the months beneath the marks you made.

3.   Make each vertical block equal to 2,500 units. Begin with 50,000 units at the bottom of the vertical scale. Label each multiple of 5,000 units in the vertical scale.

4.   Use the rounded production and sales figures from the worksheet to make the graph. Place a small dot at the point where the month and the unit production or unit sales quantity intersect. Use a dashed (---) line for production figures and a solid line (——) for sales.

PRO-IMAGE COMPANY
UNIT PRODUCTION AND SALES
Nine Months Ending September 30, 20—

     Name ____   Date ____________

Integrated Project 8, *continued*

Step Three

The Pro-Image Company reports data on a quarterly basis on employee absences that are due to illness. Complete the frequency distribution table below that shows a tally of the total number of employees absent from work on each of the workdays in the third quarter. Then use the grouped data in the table to answer the questions that follow the table.

Pro-Image Company
Employee Absence Data
Third Quarter, 20—

Number of Employees Absent from Work	Number of Times Event Occurred		Total
	Frequency		
0			
1			
2			
3			
4			
5			

1. The average number of employees absent per day was

    a.____ employees, shown as the mean, to the nearest tenth employee.

    b.____employees, shown as the median.

    c.____employees, shown as the mode.

2. As part of its employee benefits package, the Pro-Image Company pays its employees for 7 personal-leave days a year, including illness-related absences. The average daily wage of Pro-Image's employees is $98.80. If all employees were paid for the days they were absent in the third quarter, what was the total cost for absent employees' wages during the quarter?

Integrated Project 8, continued

3. Use the employee absence data from the third quarter to determine: **a.** **a.** the probability that no employees will be absent from work because of illness on any day during the next quarter. **b.** the percent of the workdays in the next quarter where all employees will be at work, rounded to the nearest percent.

4. Use the employee absence data to find the probability, stated to the nearest **tenth** percent, that no more than two employees will be absent from work during the next quarter due to illness.

Step Four

Employee wages are adjusted in the following quarter for increases in the cost of living as measured by the Consumer Price Index (CPI) during the previous quarter. During the third quarter, the CPI increased by 1%.

5. Determine the following:

   a. What hourly pay increase will the average employee get in the fourth quarter, to the nearest cent, if the average hourly pay of employees in the third quarter is $12.35?

   b. How much more would an average employee earn per week in the fourth quarter by working a 40-hour week at the new average hourly rate?

6. The average weekly wages paid by the Pro-Image Company is $39,520.

   a. How much more will the average weekly wage cost be after employee wages are adjusted for the increase in the CPI?

   b. How much will the Pro-Image Company's employee wage cost increase over the 13-week period of the fourth quarter after the employee wages are adjusted?

Lesson 9.1   *Computer Hardware and Storage*

Exercises

1. Rondel Corporation bought 34 desktop computers at $1,134 and 12 notebook computers at $1,625 from Texson, Inc. They paid $100 extra for each desktop system and $175 extra for each notebook system for an extended warranty. Find the total cost of the computers and warranty service.

2. Fleigel Sales, Inc. networks their 21 desktop computers. They pay $37,620 for a file server, $8,580 for a network printer, $3,612 for the other hardware, and $3,840 for installation of the network. **a.** Find the total cost of the hardware, installed. **b.** Find the cost of the network per desktop computer.

3. Jericho Storage, **Inc.** upgrades its computer network of 31 desktop computer systems and one server. They buy 31 **faster network** cards at $110 each, network cabling for $746, a new server for $54,890, and other devices costing $3,638. Installation took 41 hours at $115 an hour. **a.** Find the total cost of the hardware and installation. **b.** Find the cost per desktop of the upgrade.

4. Madison Community Development Corporation leased 6 notebook computers at $78.35 a month and 11 desktop computers at $39.82 a month for three years. **a.** Find the cost of leasing one notebook computer for three years. **b.** Find the cost of leasing one desktop computer for three years. **c.** Find the total cost of leasing the notebooks and desktops for three years.

        Chapter 9 *Workbook*

Lesson 9.1   *Computer Hardware and Storage*

5. A company can lease notebook computers at \$81.38 per month on a three-year lease or \$58.45 a month on a four-year lease. **a.** Find the annual cost of a notebook on a three-year lease. **b.** Find the annual cost of a notebook on a four-year lease. **c.** How much less would the company pay out per year for each notebook if they chose the 4-year leasing method.

6. The Jarold Agency can lease notebook computers from Taylor Office Rentals for \$88.24 a month each on a three-year lease basis. They can buy the same notebook computer from Wegars Office Equipment Company for \$2,257. Wegars will let them trade in each notebook for a new system at the notebook's fair market value after three years, which is estimated to be \$542. **a.** Find the cost of leasing 30 notebook computers from Taylor for three years **b.** Find the net cost of buying 30 notebooks from Wegars and using them as trade ins on new equipment at the end of three years. **c.** Name the least expensive method. **d.** Find the amount saved over a 3-year period by using the less expensive method.

7. A company wants to add hard drives to one of their file servers to make more storage space available to users of the network. They estimate that 21 users each will need 6 gigabytes of file space, 5 users require 12 gigabytes each, and 10 users will need 750 MB each. **a.** What total file space, in gigabytes, is needed? **b.** What is the average file space needed per user, in gigabytes? **c.** How many 100 GB hard drives are needed for the project?

8. A graphics firm needs to store 2.46 TB of data files including photographs and drawings. **a.** If they store the files on 250 MB removable disks, how many disks would they need? **b.** If they store the files on 650 CD-ROM disks, how many CD-ROM disks would they need? **c.** If they stored the files on 5.2 GB DVD disks, how many disks would they need?

         Chapter 9 *Workbook*

Lesson 9.2 *Software*

Exercises

1. Tundel College needs web-authoring software for 6 computers in its Recruiting Office. A commercial program the office likes retails for $89.99, and offers a 10% educational discount. The office can also buy a shareware program for $38.79 with fewer features but no educational discount. **a.** What is the cost to equip its computers with the commercial program? **b.** What is the cost to buy the shareware software? **c.** By buying shareware how much does the office would save?

2. The Mitchell Humane Society's office needs to acquire word processing and spreadsheet software for its 4 computer systems. It can buy word processing software at $129.97 a copy and spreadsheet software at $89.89 a copy. It can also buy an application suite of software that offers both programs plus presentation and database software at $475.99 a copy. **a.** What is the total amount it would spend on software if it bought the word processing and spreadsheet packages individually? **b.** What is the total amount it would spend on the application suite? **c.** How much would the office save by buying only the software needed?

3. Segal, Inc. needs to acquire antivirus software for 55 desktop computers. It could buy a 25-user license for an antivirus software package for $379.89, a 50-user license for $649.99, or single copies for $19.99 a copy. **a.** Find the per copy cost of the software with a 25-user license. **b.** Find the per copy cost of the software with a 50-user license. **c.** If they chose the 50-user license, how much would their total cost for the software for all of their computers be?

4. The Roland Corporation could develop a factory reporting system using its own information systems staff. Roland estimates that it would take 4 programmers 200 hours each to create the program. Each programmer is paid $35 an hour. Other development costs are estimated to be $18,350. They could also pay $29,560 to the B-Line Software Company to modify B-Line's existing software to fit Roland's needs. **a.** What is the estimated cost to develop the program in house? **b.** What is the amount saved by paying B-Line to modify an existing software package?

5. A programmer, paid $42 an hour, took 400 hours to develop a sales report program of 1,300 lines of computer instructions. **a.** What is the average number of finished lines per hour? **b.** What was the average programming cost per line, to the nearest cent?

Lesson 9.3 *Computer System Support*

Exercises

1. Last year, Malia Corporation upgraded each of its computer systems. Malia spent $148,850 on hardware upgrades, $107,217 on hardware replacements, and $21,658 on labor to install the hardware. It spent another $27,030 on software upgrades and $8,110 on labor to install the upgrades. The corporation had 1,060 desktop and notebook computers last year. **a.** What was the total amount they spent on hardware and software upgrades and replacements? **b.** What was the cost per computer of the upgrades and replacements, to the nearest whole dollar?

2. Sedelack, Inc. purchased a site license for software upgrades for its 320 desktop and notebook computer systems at $18,542. It took an average of 1.15 hours per computer at an average cost of $34 an hour for their technical support people to install the upgrades and reconfigure the systems. Also, the cost to retrain the 320 users to use the upgraded software was $2,500. **a.** What was the total cost of the upgrade to the company? **b.** What was the average cost of the upgrade per system, to the nearest whole dollar? **c.** What was the cost of training per user, to the nearest cent?

3. The Seybold Technical Institute has 454 computer users and 7 technical support employees. What is the ratio of technical support personnel to computer users, rounded up to the next whole person?

4. Blythe Craft Supplies, Inc. has 356 computer users. **a.** If the information systems department at Blythe wishes to provide technical support personnel in a ratio of 1 for every 50 users, what is the number of technical support personnel they need, rounded up to the next whole person? **b.** If the average weekly salary for technical support personnel is $1,230, what is the yearly salary cost for technical support personnel?

5. The Kramer Organization, a nonprofit agency, contracts with MyTechHelper, Inc. for technical support. The support firm charges $120 an hour for standard help delivered within a business day and $195 an hour for emergency help delivered within 4 hours and for weekend or holiday calls. If Kramer uses the firm for 4.75 hours of emergency help, 7.15 hours of help on a weekend, and 83.25 hours of standard help in the year, what is the total amount spend for technical support?

Lesson 9.4 *E-Business*

Exercises

1. Tennyson Corporation paid a web hosting company $45 to register its web address and $67 monthly for an Internet connection, 30 MB of server space, and 10 email addresses. Tennyson paid Clark, Inc., a web development firm, $35 an hour to develop web pages for the site and a flat fee of $30 a month to update the site. It took 21 hours for Clark to create the web site. What was the total cost of the web site for the first year?

2. Vanguard, Inc. hired BestWeb, Inc. to develop and maintain a web site for them. BestWeb charged $1,240 to develop the site, $25 annually to register its address, and $35 a month to keep the site updated. Vanguard also paid an Internet service provider $49 a month for an Internet connection. **a.** What was Vanguard's total first-year cost for the web site and Internet connection? **b.** If the total number of site hits in the first year was 51,456, find the cost per hit, to the nearest cent.

3. Using the table in Lesson 9.4 in the textbook, find the number of 128 Kbps ISDN lines needed, to the nearest whole line, to match the line capacity of one T3 connection and of one OC1 line.

4. A small office connected its network to an Internet service provider using an ISDN line. The line cost $105 a month and the hardware and software needed to make the connection cost $1,358, installed. The ISP charged $75 to set up the connection and $89 a month for unlimited use, web space, and email accounts. What was the total cost of the connection for the first year?

5. The Village Clerk's office in Glenville paid a telephone company for a fractional T1 line to connect 21 computers to an Internet service provider at a cost of $125 a month. The office also spent $2,378 to install equipment and software to make the connection. The ISP charged the firm $175 a month for the connection, some server space, and 25 email accounts. It also charged a setup fee of $275. **a.** What was the total first-year cost of the connection? **b.** What was the first-year cost per computer?

Lesson 9.5 *Wireless Communications*

Exercises

Use the cell phone and pager tables in Lesson 9.5 in the textbook to solve the Exercises 1 – 6.

1. Juan Batista uses Teffco wireless phone and service plan. His used total airtime in June was 298 minutes, of which 71 minutes were for long-distance calls and 48 minutes were made outside his home coverage area. Taxes and other charges were 12.5% of his basic monthly rate and airtime charges. Find Juan's Teffco phone bill for June.

2. If Juan, from question 1, had used Wyrless instead of Teffco, and his taxes and other charges were still 12.5%, find the amount of his phone bill for June.

3. If Juan, from question 1, had used LoadStar instead of Teffco, and his taxes and other charges were still 12.5%, find the amount of his phone bill for June.

4. Barbara Morris uses a pager that her organization rents from MetroPage. Her service includes one added paging area and voice mail service. Barbara used 425 calls during April. If April was Barbara's first month using the pager, find her paging service bill for April.

5. Julian Company has decided to rent pagers and paging service for its 21 sales representatives. The company has also decided to use MegaPage as the service provider. Julian's service included one added paging area and voice mail service. The company had to pay MegaPage in advance for the first month's service. Find the amount the Julian Company paid.

6. Lilla Woods decided to rent a pager and service from TriState Paging. Lilla also chose to have two added areas and voice mail with her service. Find Lilla's first month's charges even if she did not receive any pages at all.

Chapter 9 *Workbook*

Term Puzzler

Directions   Some of the terms listed below are in the puzzle. Circle each term when you find it. It may be written downward, upward, sideways, or diagonally. There are 17 terms in the puzzle. How many can you find?

activation fee	hit	roaming charge
airtime	home coverage area	shareware
application software	kilobyte	storage media
carrier	megabyte	TCO
cell phone service plan	OC1	terabyte
ebusiness	OC3	T1
fractional T1	operating system	T3
freeware	pager	
gigabyte	paging service plan	

```
H  I  T  C  O  E  F  O  R  E  B  U  S  I  N  E  S  F
O  P  E  R  A  T  I  N  G  S  Y  S  T  E  M  I  H  H  R
M  V  A  B  R  R  R  O  A  M  I  N  G  C  H  A  R  G  E
E  E  I  G  Q  X  R  N  I  G  E  X  X  F  R  W  E  L  E
C  M  R  D  E  M  H  I  O  C  D  G  I  E  D  J  S  P  W
O  M  T  C  K  R  J  Z  E  K  E  D  W  A  S  E  E  J  A
V  G  I  G  A  B  Y  T  E  R  U  A  W  H  N  B  T  N  R
E  T  M  X  C  K  Y  D  F  V  R  K  I  L  O  B  Y  T  E
R  A  E  S  T  O  R  A  G  E  M  E  D  I  A  E  B  V  R
A  P  P  L  I  C  A  T  I  O  N  S  O  F  T  W  A  R  E
G  F  O  C  V  G  I  I  U  K  A  T  B  X  U  S  G  O  L
E  F  T  P  A  D  J  B  W  J  O  X  D  X  F  L  E  O  Z
A  D  K  Q  T  X  Y  G  I  U  W  S  D  R  O  H  M  B  O
R  I  F  C  I  E  O  M  M  P  P  N  B  I  O  J  P  O  M
E  D  Z  O  O  X  N  C  S  M  V  A  H  B  D  X  R  P  J
A  R  F  A  N  K  X  P  P  Q  O  D  C  F  D  W  T  L  S
G  C  K  G  F  S  F  X  J  T  B  N  J  J  L  B  A  H  P
C  J  X  W  E  C  J  I  O  G  H  O  I  D  O  Z  J  F  Y
G  K  R  U  E  F  N  T  O  E  H  Y  S  K  H  U  X  C  W
```

Integrated Project 9

Directions Read through the entire project before you begin doing and work.

Step One

Ira and Rosa Feldman own and operate a temporary help agency, Helpmate, Inc. They decided to upgrade the agency's computer systems. They contracted with First Alliance Associates, Inc., a computer-consulting firm, to help them plan the new system. After reviewing the existing systems and studying the agency's needs, First Alliance recommended that Helpmate buy the following equipment to establish and connect their computers to a network: 12 PCs at $1,498, 12 network cards at $83.99, 12 network cables at $6.49, a color printer at $1,259, a laser printer at $3,989, a server at $24,899, and other network hardware at $4,216.

1. The total cost of the hardware was ____________.

2. The cost of the hardware per workstation was ____________.

Step Two

First Alliance recommended that Helpmate buy 12 operating system software packages for the PCs at $198 each and a 15-user license for network software at $2,499. They also recommended that Helpmate buy 12 copies of an office suite of software, selecting from either a popular package that costs $495 per copy, or a shareware package at $89.99 per copy.

3. The total cost of the popular package would be ___________.

4. The total cost of the shareware package would be ____________.

5. Helpmate would save ____________ by buying the shareware package rather than the popular package.

6. The total cost of the software if Helpmate buys the shareware package is ______________.

Step Three

Helpmate wants to connect their PCs to the Internet so that office staff can access e-mail and use the Web. First Alliance recommends that they use ZipNet, an ISP, and buy a 768 kbps DSL connection from their local telephone company to ZipNet. The telephone company will charge them $249 a month for the DSL connection. The installation and setup fees will be waived because of a sales promotion. ZipNet will charge $89 a month for the Internet connection and provide up to 25 e-mail accounts. Helpmate will have to buy and install $3,155 in other equipment and software for the connection. Also, First Alliance recommends that Helpmate buy a 20-user license for an antivirus software package at $695 and firewall software at $1,345.

                                                    Chapter 9 *Workbook*

Integrated Project 9, continued

7. The total cost of Helpmate's Internet connection for the first year is ______________.

8. The first-year cost of the Internet connection per workstation is ______________.

Step Four

First Alliance recommends that Helpmate hire Aegis Corporation to develop and maintain a web site. Aegis estimates that development of the web site will take 21 hours at a cost of $76 an hour. Aegis will also charge $45 annually to register Helpmate's web address and $95 a month to maintain the website.

9. The total cost of the website in the first year will be ______________.

Step Five

First Alliance recommends that Helpmate contract with Halcyon Technologies for the technical support to install, configure, and maintain their computer hardware, software, and network and to train their employees in the use of the new equipment and software. Halcyon charges $95 an hour for onsite installation and maintenance work. They also charge $1,700 a day for training of groups of less than 25 people.

10. Halcyon estimates that it will take 75 hours to install and configure the hardware and software purchased so far. The estimated cost of installing and configuring the systems is ___________.

11. Halcyon estimates that Helpmate will need, on average, 4 hours of maintenance per month during the first year. The estimated cost of maintenance during the first year is ______________.

12. After reviewing Helpmate's needs, Halcyon suggests 3 days of training for the employees. The cost of training during the first year is ______________.

Step Six

Helpmate decides to make 20 pagers available for use by their temporary help and other employees away from the home office. They contract with MetroPage (see pager service table in Lesson 9.5 in the textbook) for the rental of 20 pagers with one added area.

13. The first-year cost of the paging service, less charges for extra calls, will be ______________.

Lesson 10.1 *Employee Recruitment Costs*

Exercises

1. A newspaper charges $350 for a small ad in the classified ads section that includes help wanted listings. The same ad will cost 15% more if it appears in a special employment section. Both ad rates are daily rates. The Azure Company wants to place 4 separate ads for four job openings. **a.** What is the daily cost of one ad in the special section? **b.** What is the cost of four ads in the classifieds for one day? **c.** How much more will it cost to place four ads in the special section than in the classified section for one day?

2. A national newspaper publishes five editions, one each for five geographic areas of the U. S. A national employment ad appearing in all five editions costs $4,860 for one day. The ad could also be placed as a regional ad in one of the geographic editions at a cost of $1,045 per edition, per day. **a.** What is the cost per geographic area of a one-day national ad? **b.** How much less would one national ad cost than five regional ads in the same day? **c.** What is the total cost for placing four national ads and 12 regional ads?

3. Tech Avenue, a monthly trade publication, sells a one-eighth-page employment ad for $2,750 per issue. An advertiser who contracts for 12 ads a year pays $2,255 per ad, for the same ad. **a.** What is the rate of discount given by Tech Avenue to employers who buy an annual ad contract? **b.** What amount will Federal Tek Services pay for an annual contract of 12 ads? **c.** If Federal Tek gets an average of 25 applications per ad, what is the contract ad's cost per applicant?

4. A large corporation interviews students at 76 colleges in a year's time. The corporation places two ads, each one a week apart, in 76 college newspapers reminding students to sign up for interviews. The average cost of one-half the ads is $236, and $290 for the remaining half. **a.** What average amount per college will the corporation pay for two ads? **b.** What total amount will the corporation pay for the ads at all colleges where it interviews?

5. Maple Labs screened 27 applicants for a technician opening and selected 6 applicants for interviews. The task of screening all applicants took 4 hours at $28.50 an hour. The 6 applicants each had 30-minute telephone interviews by a manager whose interview time costs $43 an hour. Two applicants were brought in for one-day personal interviews by several staff members at a cost of $365 per day, per applicant. One applicant was offered the job and accepted it. Other costs connected with hiring the applicant totaled $820. What was the total cost of filling the lab technician opening?

Lesson 10.1 *Employee Recruitment Costs*

6. The cost of processing all applicants for a web-page designer job was $3,200. Additional hiring costs for the person selected for the job were: second-interview travel and lodging costs, $1,286; relocation expenses, $3,060; hiring expenses, $760. What was the total cost of filling the designer job?

7. Charlotte Turner, a college recruiter for Ninth Avenue Bank, hired 8 commercial loan trainees during interviews at 12 college campuses in 34 working days. Charlotte's expenses were: wages, $225 a day plus 31% in benefits; mileage, 2,100 miles at 34.5¢ a mile; lodging, $2,448; per diem expenses, at $78; incidentals, $310. **a.** What was the total cost of the recruiting trip? **b.** What was the recruiting cost per trainee hired?

8. Smith and Dean hired a director of corporate security through a recruiting firm that charged a 30% contingency fee of all first-year cash payments. The director was paid a $7,500 hiring bonus and a first-year salary of $86,000. What was the recruiting firm's fee?

9. Edwards and LaRowe are recruiters who work for competing firms that charge a contingency fee of 35% of salary. Edwards and LaRowe recruited patent attorneys for Hesson Pharmaceutical, Inc. An attorney recruited by LaRowe was selected for the job that pays $115,000 a year. **a.** What fee did LaRowe's firm collect? **b.** What fee did Edwards' firm collect?

10. An employment agency provides temporary medical staff to hospitals. The agency charges $42 an hour for nurses it places. The nurses are paid $29.40 an hour. **a.** What percent of its fee does the agency keep? **b.** What total payment would a hospital make to the agency if 3 nurses are employed 48 hours a week for 4 weeks?

11. An employment agency charges Bix Engineering $52 an hour for a construction supervisor employed on a contract basis. A construction supervisor employed full time by Bix is paid $1,665 a week plus 36% in benefits. If both the contract and full-time employees work a 52-week year, 9 hours a day, five days a week: **a.** what total amount will Bix pay the employment agency? **b.** what is the total annual cost to Bix of employing the full-time supervisor?

Lesson 10.2 *Wage and Salary Increases*

Exercises

1. Molly Rinz and Leon Szopek work for Shelby Packaging Products, Inc. Molly earns $15.65 an hour and Leon earns $14.12 an hour. On January 1, both receive a COLA of 2.8%. **a.** After the raise, what will be Molly's new pay rate? **b.** After the raise, what will be Leon's rate?

2. Cassandra Messier's gross wages last quarter were $8,500. Her employer pays a COLA equal to the 0.82% rise in the CPI during the last quarter by issuing a retroactive check to all employees. What will be the gross amount of Cassandra's retroactive check?

3. Salaried workers at Coulter & Barnes had average annual wages of $38,200 last year. On January 1, their wages were adjusted for last year's 3.7% rise in the CPI. On average, how much should salaried workers expect to earn this year if they receive no pay increases other than a COLA?

4. Clement Siegfried's hourly pay rate was $11.80 on December 31. On January 1, he received a 0.65% COLA. **a.** Find his hourly pay rate on January 1. **b.** On April 1, Clement received a 1.1% COLA. Find the increase to his hourly pay rate. **c.** Find his new pay rate on April 1.

5. For having a perfect work attendance record, Magdelena Santiago's employer paid her a bonus of 1.5% of her annual gross pay of $41,355. What was the amount of the bonus?

6. Each of six employees in the shipping department received a 5% bonus based on their suggestion that saved their employer $72,000 last year. Their average annual pay is $36,740. **a.** What average bonus did they receive? **b.** What total bonus was paid to the six employees? **c.** What percent of the amount the employer saved was paid as a bonus to the six employees, to the nearest tenth percent?

Lesson 10.2 *Wage and Salary Increases*

7. By stressing teamwork, 62 employees of Bidwell Manufacturing improved the efficiency of the factory and cut costs by $480,000. Bidwell's owner decided to give a bonus of 50% of the cost savings to his employees. **a.** What total amount will be paid in bonuses to employees? **b.** What bonus will each employee receive, to the nearest dollar?

8. Ready-Now Software, in its third year of operation, decided to give employee bonuses based on length of service. First-year employees get 2.5%, second-year employees get 4.5%, and third-year employees get 7% of their gross wages for last year. Gabriel Medina earned $72,635 last year and has been with Ready-Now since it opened for business. What bonus will Gabriel receive?

9. Gail Marketing Group shared $340,000 of its profit for the year with 28 marketing staff. What amount of profit sharing did each marketing staff member get, to the nearest dollar?

10. Arkady Restaurants sets aside 5% of its annual profits to share equally with managers of its 15 restaurants. Last year, Arkady's profit was $1,800,000. **a.** What total amount of profit will managers share? **b.** What amount of profit will each manager receive?

11. In addition to a $215,000-a-year salary, the CEO of Perkins Entertainment receives 3% of the company's annual profits. For the year, Perkins reported profits of $1,710,000. **a.** What amount of profit sharing should the CEO expect to receive? **b.** What total compensation should the CEO expect to receive for the year?

12. Two years ago, the 152 employees of Olson Glass Works received profit-sharing checks averaging $1,281. Last year 168 employees' profit-sharing checks averaged $1,762. What total amount did Olson Glass Works pay out in profit sharing in the past two years?

Lesson 10.3 *Total Cost of Labor*

Exercises

1. As a full-time employee, Rena Cole is paid an annual salary of $42,000. Her employer pays 9.2% of total wages as required benefits based on employer taxes for FICA, federal and state unemployment, and state workers' compensation. The employer also spends another 23% of wages to provide Rena with other benefits. **a.** Based on Rena's salary, how much does her employer pays in required benefits? **b.** How much does her employer pay in other benefits? **c.** What is the cost to the employer to employ Rena for one year?

2. Cully Hermann earned $38,126 last year and received 27.5% of his wages in basic benefits. In addition, Cully put $960 into an optional retirement savings plan last year. Cully's employer matches each employee's contribution to the savings program at a rate of 50%. **a.** What was the total cost of Cully's benefits to the employer? **b.** What was the employer's total annual cost of Cully's employment?

3. The total gross wages paid last year to 240 employees of Griffin Manufacturing were $10,080,000. The cost of employee benefits to Griffin was 36.3% of wages. By getting a different health insurance plan, Griffin can reduce its employee benefits cost by 1.4% of wages. **a.** What amount did Griffin spend to pay for employee benefits last year? **b.** Based on last year's wages, how much less could Griffin expect to pay for employee benefits this year because of the change in health insurance?

4. Marc Bishop worked 18 hours last week at a dry cleaning store at a pay rate of $6.65 an hour. His employer must pay these legally required taxes on Marc's pay: 7.65% FICA; unemployment tax, 3.4%; worker's compensation, 0.5%. **a.** What was the total of required taxes on Marc's pay? **b.** What was the dry cleaner's total cost of hiring Marc for the week?

5. Kinuyo Dazai works part-time giving piano lessons at a music store. The store charges students $25 for a half-hour lesson and pays Kinuyo 50% of the lesson's cost. On average, Kinuyo gives 12 lessons a week. Her employer pays legally required taxes of 10.74% of Kinuyo's gross wages. **a.** What average gross pay does Kinuyo earn a week? **b.** What required taxes must the music store pay on Kinuyo's weekly average gross pay? **c.** What is the music store's total cost of hiring Kinuyo to give 12 lessons?

Lesson 10.4 *Tracking and Reordering Inventory*

Exercises

Enter the heading and transaction data into the stock record forms and keep a running balance for Exercises 1-3.

1. Dexter Wholesale sells diced tomatoes, Stock #187-DT-300, by the case. Each case contains 48, #300 size cans of diced tomatoes. The reorder point is 30 cases. Transactions for September 1-15 follow.

9-3	Sold	96
9-6	Sold	36
9-7	Received	180
9-8	Sold	115
9-11	Sold	55
9-15	Received	210

Stock Record

Item:

Reorder Point:

Stock No: Unit:

Date	Quantity Received	Quantity Issued	Balance
8-31			141

2. St. Aubin Electrical Supply sells 14/2 insulated copper wire in 150 ft. rolls. The reorder point is 15 rolls, and the stock number is 14/2-ICPI-150. Transactions for May follow.

5-2	Received	72
5-8	Sold	30
5-12	Sold	51
5-20	Received	96
5-24	Sold	68
5-29	Sold	24

Stock Record

Item:—

Reorder Point:

Stock No: Unit:

Date	Quantity Received	Quantity Issued	Balance
4-30			12

Lesson 10.4 *Tracking and Reordering Inventory*

3. Pillar's Auto Supply sells a private brand of 48-month car batteries, Stock # 48BAT-2X, and keeps a record of each battery sold. The reorder point is 20 batteries. Transactions for December 1-7 follow.

12-1	Sold	42
12-2	Sold	36
12-3	Sold	53
12-4	Received	120
12-4	Sold	36
12-5	Sold	38
12-6	Sold	44
12-7	Sold	21

Stock Record			
Item:		Reorder Point:	
Stock No.		Unit:	
Date	Quantity Received	Quantity Issued	Balance
11-30			150

4. Deer Park Office Supply sells 1,800 cases of copy paper every 30 days. Lead time to replenish stock is 3 days. Safety stock of copy paper is 40 cases. **a.** How many cases of paper are used daily? **b.** What is the reorder point?

5. A furniture company uses 13,200 corrugated boxes in 22 working days. It takes 2 days' lead time to get more boxes. Safety stock is 900 boxes. **a.** How many boxes are used daily? **b.** What is the reorder point?

6. In 88 working days during the first quarter, Midwell Cabinets used 91,520 custom cabinet hinges. Lead time for hinges is 7 days. Midwell keeps safety stock of 2,500 hinges. **a.** What is the daily use of hinges? **b.** What is the reorder point for hinges, to the nearest thousand?

7. A trophy store uses 18,720 metal engraving plates, size 0.75" × 5", a year. The store is open 6 days a week, 52 weeks a year. Lead time for delivery of new plates is 6 days. Safety stock is 100 plates. **a.** What is the daily plate usage? **b.** What is the reorder point for plates, to the nearest hundred?

Lesson 10.5 *Inventory Valuation*

Exercises

A wholesaler's inventory records for cases of paper towels and tub and tile cleaner are shown. For both products, find the total value of the ending inventory, to the nearest cent, for each inventory method listed. Where required, also find the unit cost of the ending inventory.

Inventory Record					
Stock Item: Paper Towel, Case				Stock # 2138-T	
Date	**Transaction**	**Units**	**Unit Cost**	**Total Value**	
11-1	Beginning Inventory	180	$55.80	$10,044.00	
11-6	Purchase	350	54.72	19,152.00	
11-12	Purchase	425	53.28	22,644.00	
11-20	Purchase	275	56.16	15,444.00	
11-29	Purchase	190	64.80	12,312.00	
11-30	Ending Inventory	210			

1. Using FIFO, find the value of the ending inventory for paper towels.

Inventory Record					
Stock Item: Tub and Tile Cleaner, Case				Stock # A-427-TX	
Date	**Transaction**	**Units**	**Unit Cost**	**Total Value**	
3-1	Beginning Inventory	207	$85.92	$17,785.44	
3-2	Purchase	640	79.20	50,688.00	
3-11	Purchase	190	87.36	16,598.40	
3-18	Purchase	320	84.00	26,880.00	
3-25	Purchase	410	82.56	33,849.60	
3-30	Purchase	140	88.32	12,364.80	
3-31	Ending Inventory	301			

2. Using LIFO, find the value of the ending inventory.

3. **a.** Using the weighted average method and rounding to the nearest cent, find the average unit cost of the ending inventory. **b.** What is the value of the ending inventory?

4. Using FIFO, find the value of the ending inventory for tub and tile cleaner.

5. Using LIFO, find the value of the ending inventory.

6. **a.** Using the weighted average method and rounding to the nearest cent, find the average unit cost of the ending inventory. **b.** What is the value of the ending inventory?

Lesson 10.5 *Inventory Valuation*

The Bryson Company's inventory records of two parts used to produce vacuum cleaners are shown below. The brush and cord assemblies are stored until they are issued to the manufacturing division. For both parts, find the value of the ending inventory for each inventory method listed, to the nearest cent. Where required, find the unit cost of the ending inventory. Note that the ending inventory is not given and will have to be calculated.

7. What is the ending inventory, in units?

Inventory Record				
Stock Item: Brush Assembly			**Stock # BR-12-Z**	
Date	**Transaction**	**Units**	**Unit Cost**	**Total Value**
2-1	Beginning Inventory	152	$6.62	$1,006.24
2-1	Received	800	6.55	5,240.00
2-8	Received	700	6.60	4,620.00
2-15	Received	1,200	6.40	7,680.00
2-22	Received	450	6.75	3,037.50
2-28	Issued This Month	2,582		
2-28	Ending Inventory			

8. Using FIFO, what is the value of the ending inventory of brush assemblies?

9. Using LIFO, what is the value of the ending inventory?

10. a. Using the weighted average method and rounding to the nearest cent, what is the average unit cost of the ending inventory? **b.** What is the value of the ending inventory?

11. What is the ending inventory, in units?

Inventory Record				
Part: Cord Assembly			**Part # SW/A27**	
Date	**Transaction**	**Units**	**Unit Cost**	**Total Value**
2-1	Beginning Inventory	554	$8.15	$4,515.10
2-1	Received	900	8.12	7,308.00
2-9	Received	1,600	8.05	12,880.00
2-16	Received	520	8.19	4,258.80
2-23	Received	240	8.22	1,972.80
2-28	Issued This Month	2,948		
2-28	Ending Inventory			

12. Using FIFO, what is the value of the ending inventory of cord assemblies?

13. Using LIFO, what is the value of the ending inventory?

14. a. Using the weighted average method and rounding to the nearest cent, what is the average unit cost of the ending inventory? **b.** What is the value of the ending inventory?

Chapter 10 *Workbo*

Lesson 10.6 *Ordering and Carrying Inventory*

Exercises

1. Classic Footwear, a shoe store chain, issues 6,800 purchase orders a year. A product manager and two assistants devote 55% of their time to ordering and 45% to other purchasing tasks. Their gross compensation including benefits is $135,000 a year. Nineteen percent of annual warehouse costs of $230,000 and 20% of annual office costs of $84,000 are charged to purchasing.   **a.** What amount of gross compensation is spent on ordering? **b.** What total amount is spent on purchasing? **c.** What is the average cost of issuing purchase orders, to the nearest cent?

2. These costs of buying merchandise for the LaRue Clothing Company are allocated to purchasing in the percentages shown: 46% of $281,000 in office labor costs; 8% of $589,000 in overhead costs; 15% of $786,000 in warehouse costs. Computer costs are allocated at $1.27 per purchase order. LaRue Clothing issued 19,500 purchase orders last year. The allocation to purchasing for each cost category is: **a.** labor; **b.** overhead; **c.** warehouse. **d.** What were the total computer costs for purchase orders? **e.** What was the total cost of purchasing? **f.** What was the cost per purchase order issued, to the nearest cent?

3. Zigwell Manufacturing spent an average of $18 per order to issue 30,000 purchase orders last year. Of the cost per order, 60% was related to office and warehouse wage costs, 21% to office costs, 6% to overhead, and 13% to warehouse costs. Zigwell estimates that all wage costs will increase 4.6% this year and all other costs of purchasing will increase 2.1%.   **a.** What are the total estimated purchasing costs for this year? **b.** If the same number of purchase orders is issued this year as last year, what is the estimated cost per purchase order, to the nearest cent?

Lesson 10.6 *Ordering and Carrying Inventory*

4. The Buchanan Window Company finances 80% of its annual inventory value of $6,000,000 at an interest rate of 8.6%. It also pays a personal property tax of 0.85% of the inventory's annual value. Other costs of carrying the inventory are: labor, $212,000; insurance, $73,000; overhead, $98,000. **a.** What is the total annual cost of carrying the inventory? **b.** What is the cost per dollar of carrying the inventory, to the nearest tenth of a cent?

5. A store in a mall sells seasonal, special-promotion merchandise, such as flowerpots for the gardening season, autumn home decorations, Halloween decorations, and calendars. The average monthly value of inventory is $45,000. Interest costs at a 10.7% annual rate are paid on 95% of the inventory's value. Ten percent of inventory is boxed and stored for sale the following year at a storage cost of 3.8% of inventory value. Other carrying costs total $1,850 a month. **a.** What are the store's annual interest costs? **b.** Storage costs? **c.** What are the store's total annual carrying costs? **d.** What is the carrying cost per dollar of inventory, to the nearest tenth of a cent?

Term Puzzler

Complete the crossword puzzle below. Some answers are two words placed together without space between them.

Across

1. Emergency stock
4. Number of items sold divided by number of selling days
6. An always up-to-date inventory system
11. Order placed when this quantity is reached
12. Assumes stock bought first is used first
14. Amount recruiter is paid only for successful search

Down

2. Federal tax on first $7,000 of employee wages
3. Employee usually not paid overtime
5. Stock on hand
7. Type of pay for time worked in past
8. Employee hired through employment agency
9. Assumes most recent stock is used first
10. Amount paid employees for good work
13. General costs of producing or selling
14. Pay raise based on CPI

Integrated Project 10

Directions Read through the entire project before you begin doing any work.

Elisabeth Tarrillion, a management consultant, was hired by Shoe Crafter, Inc. to analyze data provided by the Human Resource, Budget, Accounting, and Payroll Departments. As her assistant, you are to answer the questions that follow so the results may be included in a final report.

Step One

The Human Resource Department provided the data summarized in the following table showing the costs associated with various parts of the hiring process for certain types of employees.

Shoe Crafter, Inc.
Average Hiring Cost, Per Hire, By Category

Cost Category	Employee Type		
	Nonexempt	Exempt, Regular	Exempt, Supervisory
Ads	$480	$1,650	$2,530
Outside Agency Fees	None	$2,500	$5,800
Travel of Recruiter and Applicant	None	$1,240	$4,600
Relocation	None	$3,200	$21,780
Interview	3 Hours @ $52	8 Hours @ $68	16 Hours @ $79
Other Hiring Costs	3 Hours @ $29	3 Hours @ $29	6 Hours @ $36

1. Find the average cost of hiring a nonexempt employee.

2. Find the average cost of hiring an exempt, regular employee.

3. Find the average cost of hiring an exempt, supervisory employee.

Step Two

The Human Resource Department reports that Shoe Crafter uses outside agencies to recruit employees for executive staff positions and to obtain temporary help for special projects.

Integrated Project 10, continued

4. Crestwood, Inc., an executive recruiting firm, conducted a successful search for a Chief Financial Officer (CFO) for Shoe Crafter. Their fee was 30% of all first-year cash compensation. In the first year, the CFO will receive a salary of $128,000, a signing bonus of $25,000, and a one-time cash payment of $32,000 to be used for relocation expenses. Beginning with the second full year of employment, the new CFO will receive options that will allow the purchase of stock with an estimated value of $30,000. What total fee will be paid to Crestwood?

5. Shoe Crafter agreed to hire contract employees from Patterson Associates, a temporary help agency, to develop an online order system at a daily cost of $341 per contract employee. Eight contract employees worked 5 days a week for 26 weeks to develop the order system. Five contract employees worked another 14 weeks to test the system and train Shoe Crafter's employees. Only two of the contract employees were kept for another 8 weeks to provide consultant service and do troubleshooting. Find the cost of:
a. development; **b.** testing and training; **c.** consultant service and troubleshooting.

Step Three
The Budget, Accounting, and Payroll Departments provided data regarding bonus and COLA payments and benefit information.

6. An employee suggestion submitted by four Shipping Department employees resulted in an estimated $7,900 monthly cost savings. Shoe Crafter decided to pay a total bonus to these employees of 40% of the estimated savings for one year. **a.** What total amount will be paid to the four employees as a bonus?
b. What bonus amount will each employee receive?

7. The CPI for the last quarter showed a 1.96% increase from the previous quarter. Shoe Crafter pays a COLA quarterly based on changes in the CPI. The total payroll for the last quarter of the 300 employees eligible to receive a COLA was $3,150,000. Based on last quarter's payroll, what amount more will be spent on payroll for a quarter after the COLA is calculated?

8. The 300 full-time nonexempt employees earned average annual gross pay of $42,000 last year. Their benefits breakdown is: legally-required payments, 8.8%; health insurance, 8.7%; retirement plan, 5.2%; personal time off (holidays, vacations, sick leave), 7.6%; life insurance, 0.3%; miscellaneous, 2.4%. **a.** What total percent of gross pay did production employees receive as benefits? **b.** What amount did the average nonexempt employee receive in total benefits last year? **c.** What amount did they receive in total benefits excluding those legally required?

Integrated Project 10, continued

Step Four

The Accounting Department provided ordering and inventory data. The table below lists the units produced and their unit production cost for the last six months of the year. Units produced become part of inventory. The inventory at the close of business on June 30 was 85,120 units with a total value of $3,064,320. The ending inventory as of December 31 was 136,000 units. Complete the table by finding the total value of production (inventory) for each month.

9.   Shoe Crafter uses FIFO. What was the value of the ending inventory?

Shoe Crafter, Inc.
Production and Production Cost Data
July 1 to December 31, 20--

Month	Units Produced	Average Unit Production Cost	Total Value
July	130,060	$34.90	
August	131,300	$34.80	
September	133,760	$34.50	
October	134,850	$34.42	
November	125,900	$35.50	
December	97,820	$40.40	

10.   If Shoe Crafter had used LIFO, what would have been the value of its ending inventory?

11.   Calculate these figures using the weighted average method of valuing inventory: **a.** total units in inventory and available for sale July 1 through December 31; **b.** unit value of inventory, to the nearest cent; **c.** value of ending inventory.

12.   The average monthly inventory was $4,500,000 last year, and 60% of average inventory was financed with loans at 12% annual interest. Insurance costs were $460,000 for the year. General storage and handling costs were estimated to be 4.5¢ of each dollar of inventory. What was the carrying cost of inventory per dollar of inventory, to the nearest tenth of a cent?

Lesson 11.1 *Manufacturing Costs*

Exercises

1. During March, the manufacturing costs of Solia Copper Products were: raw materials, $1,037,293; direct labor, $1,218,421; and factory overhead, $396,252. **a.** What was the prime cost of the goods produced? **b.** What was the total manufacturing cost of the goods produced?

2. The costs to make 2,880 footballs are: raw materials, $9,100; direct labor, $6,250; factory overhead, $1,456. **a.** What is the prime cost of the footballs? **b.** What is the total manufacturing cost? **c.** What is the manufacturing cost per football?

3. A factory had these overhead expenses for one month: supervisory wages, $328,215; rent, $22,708; depreciation, $64,128; utilities, $21,667; maintenance, $32,609; other, $11,364. What was the total factory overhead?

4. The direct costs of producing a product at a factory are: raw materials, $17,512 and direct labor, $10,700. Factory overhead is estimated at 15% of prime cost. What is the total manufacturing cost for making the product?

5. Miralo Manufacturing Corporation employs 640 people and spends $32,400 a month on its Human Resource Department. Miralo charges its other departments for human resource services on the basis of the number of employees in each department. What was the amount charged monthly for human resource services to the Assembly Department, which has 180 workers?

6. The Torrel Storage Company paid $225,600 last year to rent its factory. The factory has an area of 30,000 sq. ft. divided into these three departments: Hard Drives, 10,000 sq. ft.; Removable Media Drives, 8,000 sq. ft.; Media, 12,000 sq. ft. Rent is distributed on the basis of space. Find the amount of rent that was distributed to the: **a.** Hard Drives Department? **b.** Removable Media Department? **c.** Media Department?

Lesson 11.2 *Break-Even Point*

Exercises

1. Shelby Clothing Fashions, Inc. wants to sell tee shirts for $16 each. To do so, it estimates that manufacturing will require fixed expenses of $20,000 and variable expenses of $6 a shirt. **a.** What is the break-even point in units produced? **b.** What is the break-even point in dollar sales?

2. Tectron Co.'s fixed costs to produce hubs for computer networks are $800,000. The variable cost to produce each hub is $16. They will price the hubs at $80. **a.** How many hubs must they sell to break even? **b.** What are the sales they must reach to break even?

3. Donner Corporation estimates that to produce wooden baseball bats, it must spend $38,160 in fixed costs. The company estimates that the variable costs will be $14.89 for each bat. The selling price of the bats is to be $50.89 each. **a.** At that selling price, how many of the bats must be sold to break even? **b.** To break even, the company must have a sales income of what amount from this operation?

4. Vernon Manufacturing Company, Inc. expects to make end tables and sell them at $45 each. It estimates the fixed costs to produce the tables at $175,000 and variable costs of $20 per table. **a.** What number of tables must Vernon Manufacturing sell to break even? **b.** What is the total amount of sales it must reach to break even? **c.** If the company sells 10,000 tables, what is the amount by which the sales will exceed the break-even point?

5. Peleon Corporation wants to manufacture and sell 37,500 office scanners. It estimates fixed costs will be $1,875,000 and variable costs, $2,450,000. What is the price, rounded to the nearest cent, at which each scanner must be sold to break even?

Lesson 11.3 *Depreciation Costs*

Exercises

1. A stamping machine that costs $160,000 is depreciated 10% per year by the declining-balance method. What will be its book value at the end of three years?

2. Dill Office Support, Inc. buys a fleet of twelve delivery vans. The vans cost a total of $180,000. After three years, the vans will be traded in for their book value. Using the declining-balance method and a 30% depreciation rate, what will be the total book value of the vans at the end of three years?

3. Roberts Theatre Company buys 10 desktop computers for a total cost of $15,000. It plans to sell or trade them after five years for $3,000. Using the sum-of-the-years-digits method, what will be the book value of the computers at the end of two years?

4. Barnes Publishing Company buys three printers for its office for a total cost of $24,000. It plans to use them for four years and then trade them in for $8,000. **a.** Using the sum-of-the-years-digits method, find the amount of depreciation for the first year; **b.** second year; **c.** third year; **d.** fourth year; **e.** What will be the total depreciation for four years? **f.** What will be the book value at the end of four years?

Lesson 11.3 *Depreciation Costs*

5. Holyoke, Inc. buys lathes for $85,000. The firm plans to use the lathes for five years and then trade them in for $25,000. Using the sum-of-the-years-digits method, what is the total amount the lathes will depreciate the first three years?

6. Trenton Forms, Inc. bought a cutting press for $125,000. The press had a class life of 5 years. **a.** Using the MACRS method of depreciation, what was the maximum depreciation allowable on the press for the first year? **b.** for the third year? **c.** for the fifth year?

7. Garcia Bros., Inc. bought a new truck for their business for $22,500. It has a 5-year class life. Using the MACRS method of depreciation, what is the book value of the truck at the end of the second year?

8. Manson Corporation bought three network servers that cost a total of $145,000 and had a 5-year class life. **a.** Using the MACRS depreciation method, what was the amount of the first-year depreciation? **b.** for the second year? **c.** for the third year? **d.** At the end of the third year, what was the book value of the servers?

Lesson 11.4 *Shipping Costs*

Exercises

Use the National Shipping Company rate table on page 481 of the textbook to solve Exercises 1 – 10.

	Weight in Pounds	Destination in Zone	Shipping Charge		Weight	Destination in Zone	Shipping Charge
1.	3	2		**2.**	$10\frac{1}{2}$ lbs	2	
3.	11	8		**4.**	6 lbs	7	
5.	12	6		**6.**	4 lbs 4 oz	4	
7.	7.5	4		**8.**	2 lbs 8 oz	6	
9.	5	3		**10.**	12 lbs 3 oz	1	

11. A shipper charges $1.75 per pound to deliver a 3-pound package. Insurance costs an additional $0.45 per $100, or fraction of $100 of value. The company values its parcel at $350. What is the total cost to ship the package?

Use the Curry Freight and Express rate table on page 482 of the textbook to solve Exercises 12 – 21.

	Weight in Pounds	Destination in Zone	Freight Charge		Weight in Pounds	Destination in Zone	Freight Charge
12.	210	3		**13.**	627	1	
14.	731	8		**15.**	458	8	
16.	1,003	5		**17.**	322	6	
18.	187	6		**19.**	519	7	
20.	2,047	2		**21.**	1,828	4	

22. Rensor Pipe Manufacturing, Inc. of Adams ships 6,125 pounds of iron pipe by freight to T-Bar Corporation of Springfield, f.o.b. Adams. The freight company charges $10.25 a cwt. What is the freight charge and who pays it?

     Chapter 11 *Workbook*

Lesson 11.5 *Office Costs*

E x e r c i s e s

1. Timmerman Realty rents space for a regional office at $1,980 a month. The office is 50 feet long × 30 feet wide. **a.** How many square feet of space office does the firm rent? **b.** What is the annual rental cost of the space per square foot?

2. The trust department of a bank occupies part of the second floor of an office building and has an area of 1,260 ft². The office costs are $28,560 a year in rent, $3,432 in utilities, and $1,824 in maintenance. **a.** What is the annual cost of the office per square foot, to the nearest dollar? **b.** Using the rounded annual square foot cost you found in part a, what is the annual cost of a trust officer's office that is 50 ft² in area?

3. As part of his job, a clerk in a college recruiting office examines and verifies student application folders for completeness. The clerk can examine and verify a folder every three minutes. **a.** At that rate, how many folders can the clerk process in a $7\frac{1}{2}$ hour day? **b.** At a wage rate of $10.60 per hour, what is the cost to process each folder?

4. A department of an accounting firm has five offices. The average costs of each office are: salaries, $2,150 a month; benefits, 28% of wages; space, 120 square feet @ $31.50 per square foot per year; supplies, $325 per year; other costs, $1,830 per year. What is the total yearly cost of the five offices?

5. An order center estimates that the costs of workstations for ten order clerks and a supervisor last year were: wages and fringe benefits, $253,000; office space, $11,210; power, $1,480; depreciation, $15,200; supplies, postage, and telephone, $9,150. **a.** What is the average cost of each workstation? **b.** If the office was open 250 days last year, what was the cost of each workstation per working day? **c.** If each clerk completed 70 orders each day on average, what is the cost of each order, to the nearest cent?

                                                              Chapter 11 *Workbook*

Lesson 11.6 *Travel Expenses*

Exercises

1. Marianne Guterez ran her car 18,286 miles last year. Of those miles, 38% were for her job as a warranty repair person for a kitchen appliance company. The company reimbursed Marianne $0.345 a mile for the business use of her car. How much did Marianne receive as reimbursement for the use of her car in the last year?

2. Ted Ivany put 23,568 miles on his car last year, of which 41% were for his job as regional supervisor of store operations for Bideke, Inc. Bideke reimbursed Ted at the rate of $0.38 per mile for the business use of his car. How much did Ted receive as reimbursement for the business use of his car last year?

3. Valerie Masse added 24,906 miles to her car last year. Of those miles, 37% were reimbursed by her company at $0.32 $\frac{1}{2}$ a mile. The IRS mileage rate for that year was $0.35 a mile. **a.** How much did Valerie receive from her company for mileage? **b.** How much might Valerie use as a tax deduction?

4. Charlene Yin managed a sales booth at a conference for her firm. Her company reimbursed her for $419 in airfare, $228 for meals, $389 for customer entertainment, $72 for parking, $425 for conference registration fees, $674 for her hotel suite, and $276 in other expenses. How much did Charlene receive from her company as reimbursement?

5. Daryn White attended a conference for his company. His approved expenses were: airfare, $652; meals, $257; taxis, $29; airport parking, $52; porterage, $18; conference registration fee, $375; mileage to and from airport, 82 miles; hotel charges, $288; other expenses, $124. His company pays $0.34 a mile for use of personal cars. How much was Daryn reimbursed?

6. Luanda Marliana was away for $5\frac{1}{2}$ days at a business conference. She was reimbursed for traveling the 425 miles to and from the conference by personal car at $0.37 a mile. She was also paid $137 per diem. Find her total reimbursement for the conference.

Name ____ Date ___________

Term Puzzler

Complete the crossword puzzle below. Some answers are two or three words placed together without space between them.

Across

2. Tips for carrying bags
6. Occur no matter how much is produced
7. Wages of workers who produce products
8. Uses fixed rate of depreciation
12. Pay back
13. Expenses not tied directly to producing goods
14. When sales income equals cost of producing and selling product

Down

1. Distance from central point
3. Cwt
4. Must be used to depreciate for tax purposes
5. Measures box around thickest part
9. How long IRS lets property be depreciated
10. Cost of raw materials plus direct labor
11. Original cost less depreciation to date

Integrated Project 11

Directions Read through the entire project before you begin doing any work.

Northern Woods Corporation (NWC) manufactures outdoor furniture. It sells the furniture mainly to catalog and e-business distributors. NWC has a large staff of salespersons that visit customers to sell them furniture. At the main office, they have a smaller staff of order clerks who process orders for furniture that the salespeople phone in from the field.

One of NWC's lines of furniture is made of cedar and it has been very popular. Because of the popularity of their cedar furniture, NWC has grown rapidly in the last few years, and so have their costs of doing business. To reduce costs, NWC's management needs to study cost and income data for the firm. They have asked you to help them collect the data they need. Use the data in the exercises to calculate the answers to each question.

1. The factory records of NWC show these costs for the last quarter: raw materials, $214,378; direct labor, $605,177; supervisory salaries and wages, $74,589; rent, $29,156; depreciation and repairs, $23,056; utilities, $11,315; factory supplies, $6,373; other factory expenses, $4,116. **a.** What was NWC's prime cost of manufacturing for the quarter? **b.** What was NWC's total factory overhead for the quarter? **c.** What was NWC's total manufacturing cost for the quarter?

2. Based on the quarterly data in Exercise 1, find the percent of total manufacturing cost, to the nearest whole percent, represented by: **a.** raw materials; **b.** direct labor; **c.** factory overhead.

3. NWC pays $372,500 in salaries a year to its managers. This expense is charged to the departments of NWC on the basis of the number of workers in each department. The number of workers in each department is: Shipping and Receiving, 20; Assembly 36; Fabrication, 40; Finishing, 24. Find the amount of management salaries that should be charged to: **a.** Shipping and Receiving; **b.** Assembly; **c.** Fabrication; **d.** Finishing.

4. The company is considering adding a cedar picnic table to its line of furniture. NWC estimates that the table will sell for $40 to distributors. They also estimate that the fixed costs of producing the table will be $12,000 and that the variable costs per table will be $21. **a.** How many tables, rounded up to the next whole table, will they need to sell to break even? **b.** Find the total sales they need to break even.

Integrated Project 11, continued

5. NWC recently bought a truck for $24,500. The truck has a class life of 5 years. **a.** Using MACRS, find the total depreciation that will be allowed to be taken on the truck for the first year. **b.** Find the book value of the truck at the end of the first year.

6. NWC knows, on average, each order clerk receives and processes 48 sales orders in an 8-hour day. The order clerks make an average of $10.50 an hour. What is the average cost of order clerk wages per sales order?

7. Each order clerk's workstation occupies 60 square feet of space. NWC estimates these expenses for each order clerk's workstation: rent at $16 per square foot per year; telephone costs of $300 per month; supplies, $325 per year; depreciation of equipment, $2,100 a year; utilities, $98 a month; maintenance and insurance, $39 a month. **a.** What is the total cost of each order clerk's workstation space per year? **b.** What is the annual cost of each workstation per square foot?

8. NWC, which is located in Melville, sold 125 of its lawn chairs @ $32 to Value Gardens, Inc., a distributor who sells through both its web site and catalogs. The total weight of the shipment was 2,875 pounds. Freight charges were $34.89 per cwt or remaining fraction, f.o.b. Melville. Insurance on the shipment was $0.45 per $100 or remaining fraction of value. **a.** Find the freight charges. **b.** What is the cost of insurance? **c.** Find the total cost of the shipment. **d.** What company paid the shipping costs?

9. NWC decided to send Jill Boland, Plant Manager, to the National Association of Outdoor Furniture Manufacturers convention to attend seminars on manufacturing cost control. On her return, Jill reported these expenses: mileage to and from airport, 54 miles; airfare, $429; meals, $221; taxis, $29; airport parking, $36; porterage and other tips, $16; registration fee, $325; hotel room, $328; other expenses, $12.50. NWC's mileage reimbursement rate is $0.34 per mile. How much was Jill reimbursed for her travel expenses?

     Chapter 11 *Workbook*

Lesson 12.1   *Cash Sales and Sales on Account*

Exercises

Complete a cash proof form and find the amount of cash over or short for Exercises 1 – 4.

1. You are a cashier at Segan's Diner. You started work with a $100 change fund. At the end of your work period, the register readings show cash received, $2,473.42, and cash paid out, $25.03. Cash in the register drawer totaled $2,546.59.

2. You are a cashier at Ying's Creations. You began work with a $75 change fund. At the end of your morning work period, the register counters showed cash received, $973.22, and cash paid out, $18.20. The cash in the register drawer was $1,028.98.

3. You are a cashier at Tell's Card Shop. On Thursday, you started work with a change fund of $80. At the end of the day, the register totals showed $535.85 cash received and $8.15 cash paid out. The money in the drawer included 31 pennies, 23 nickels, 48 dimes, 60 quarters, 32 one-dollar bills, 8 five-dollar bills, 18 ten-dollar bills, 15 twenty-dollar bills, and $35.78 in checks.

4. You are a cashier at Nathan's Photo. The register had a change fund of $125 at the start of your work period. At the end of the day, the register totals were $1,665.06 cash received and $38.17 cash paid out. The money in the drawer included 121 pennies, 127 nickels, 153 dimes, 85 quarters, 61 dollars, 16 five-dollar bills, 12 ten-dollar bills, 72 twenty-dollar bills, and $8.53 in checks.

Cash Proof		
Segan's Diner	11/9/20--	
Change fund		
+ Register total of cash received		
Total		
- Register total of cash paid out		
Cash that should be in drawer		
Cash actually in drawer		
Cash short		
Cash over		

Cash Proof		
Ying's Creations	7/15/20--	
Change fund		
+ Register total of cash received		
Total		
- Register total of cash paid out		
Cash that should be in drawer		
Cash actually in drawer		
Cash short		
Cash over		

Cash Proof		
Tell's Card Shop	2/7/20--	
Change fund		
+ Register total of cash received		
Total		
- Register total of cash paid out		
Cash that should be in drawer		
Cash actually in drawer		
Cash short		
Cash over		

Cash Proof		
Nathan's Photo	10/28/20--	
Change fund		
+ Register total of cash received		
Total		
- Register total of cash paid out		
Cash that should be in drawer		
Cash actually in drawer		
Cash short		
Cash over		

Chapter 12 *Workbook*

Lesson 12 *Cash Sales and Sales on Account*

5. Moore Distributing sold the following items on Invoice 35-272, dated June 21, 20--, to Mill Home Outlet: 12-volt air compressors, stock number AC23-12V, 70 units @ $25.90; rechargeable spotlights, stock number RC-282-6, 120 units @$18.12; 8-inch × 10-inch wood picture frames, stock number, F-W-87-8/10, 65 units @ $8.41; cordless drills, stock number PT-CD1/4, 90 @ $41.65. The credit terms are n/45. Shipment is by truck. Mill Home Outlet's account number is 34-28476. Complete the invoice shown below. Calculate the extensions and the invoice total and write these amounts on the invoice.

Moore Distributing
4100 Grant Avenue
Raleigh, NC 27607-3534

Invoice:

Account No.

Sold to:Mill Home Outlet
4297 Oberlin Road
Raleigh, NC 27068-8685

Date:

Ship Via:

Terms:

Quantity	Stock No.	Description	Unit Price	Total
		Total		

6. Of the items purchased by Mill Home Outlet from Moore Distributing on Invoice 35-272, these items were returned for credit on July 3: 15 picture frames that were damaged because of improper packing; 5 air compressors because the wrong model was sent. Complete the credit memo that Moore will send to Mill Home Outlet.

Credit Memo

Moore Distributing
4100 Grant Avenue
Raleigh, NC 27607-3534

To: Mill Home Outlet
4297 Oberlin Road
Raleigh, NC 27068-8685

Account No.:

Date:

We have credited your account as follows:

Description	Unit Price	Total
Total Credit		

Lesson 12.1 *Cash Sales and Sales on Account*

7. Hoover Supplies, Inc. keeps records of customer account balances. Update their account with TMR Enterprises shown below by recording the transactions for November and finding balances.

Nov. 7 Sold TMR $6,526.40 in merchandise on sales invoice No. 4936

Nov. 13 TMR returned $193.52 of goods from invoice No. 4936; credit memo 577.

Nov. 17 TMR paid the November 1 balance of $9,324.09.

Nov. 20 TMR paid invoice No. 4936, less credit memo 577.

Nov. 22 Sold TMR $5,002.65 in merchandise on sales invoice No. 5066.

Nov. 25 TMR returned $202.91 of goods from invoice No. 5066; credit memo 621.

Account: TMR Enterprises 9127 Englewood Avenue Yakima, WA 98908-1425			Account No.: 10-2234-5	
Date	**Description**	**Charges**	**Credits**	**Balance**
11/1	Balance Forward			9,324.09

8. Vasquez Imports' customer account form with Keeble Gifts is shown below. Record Keeble's April 1 account balance of $2,383.94 and the transactions for April. Take a balance after each entry.

April 4 Sold Keeble $4,582.32 in merchandise on Invoice #1302.

April 11 Credit Memo #874 sent to Keeble for $89.67; Invoice #1302 merchandise returns.

April 15 Sold Keeble $1,892.33 in merchandise on Invoice #1387.

April 21 Received payment from Keeble for balance brought forward to April 1.

April 24 Received Keeble's payment for Invoice #1302, less Credit Memo #874.

April 28 Sold Keeble $4,190.87 in merchandise on Invoice #1516.

April 29 Received Keeble payment for Invoice #1387.

Account: Keeble Gifts 3982 East Way Blvd. Pompano Beach, FL 33072-2804			Account No.: 10-1684-3	
Date	**Description**	**Charges**	**Credits**	**Balance**

Lesson 12.2 *Cash and Trade Discounts*

Exercises

1. For each invoice, find the last date on which an invoice is due and a cash discount may be taken. Also find the amount of cash discount that may be taken on the date the invoice is paid, and the cash price.

	Invoice Amount	Invoice Date	Credit Terms	Discount Date	Due Date	Date Paid	Cash Discount	Cash Price
a.	$1,400	Jan. 5	1/10, n/30			Jan. 13		
b.	$870	Mar. 12	2/15, n/60			Mar. 27		
c.	$580	Nov. 17	1/15, n/45			Dec. 21		
d.	$12,930	Aug. 28	3/10, n/20			Sep. 1		
e.	$6,210	Dec. 6	n/14 EOM			Dec. 31		
f.	$3,725	Sep. 21	4/5, n/21			Sep 22		

2. Hansen Manufacturing sells a lawn edger to Jackie's Hardware for $140, less a 35% trade discount. **a.** What amount of trade discount is given on the edger? **b.** What is the invoice price of the edger?

3. To move stock before a new model is introduced, a supplier gives a 57% trade discount on an inkjet printer with a list price of $195. **a.** What is the trade discount amount? **b.** What is the invoice price of the printer?

4. A manufacturer offers to sell large retailers a ready-to-assemble bookcase for $37.20. The list price of the bookcase is $62. What rate of trade discount is given on the bookcase?

5. A car floor mat with a suggested retail price of $18 is offered to a supplier at a price of $11.25. What rate of trade discount is offered on the floor mat?

6. The list price of a rocker is $155. The rocker is offered to a retailer at a 45% trade discount with credit terms of 3/20, n/60. **a.** What is the invoice price of the rocker? **b.** What is the cash price of the rocker if the invoice is paid within the discount period?

Name ____ Date ____________

Lesson 12.3 *Series Trade Discounts*

Exercises

1. Bascomb's Furnishings buys a mirror listed at $236 less discounts of 20%, 10%, and 5%. What is the invoice price of the mirror?

2. An oriental rug lists at $680 with discounts to the retailer of 40% and 12%. **a.** How much does the rug costs the dealer? **b.** What is the total trade discount?

3. The list price of an electric guitar is $450. Dealers may buy the guitar at a discount of $33\frac{1}{3}\%$, 15%, and 6%. What is the invoice price of the electric guitar?

 Name _____________________________________ Date _____________

Lesson 12.3 *Series Trade Discounts*

4. A retailer may buy a chain saw from Chessler Products for $180 less 25% and 5%. The same saw may be purchased from Elger Supply Company for $204 less 20%, 10%, and 15%. What is the invoice price of the saw: **a.** from Chessler? **b.** from Elger? **c.** By buying at the lower price, how much can the retailer save per saw?

5. Use the percent method to find the single discount that is equivalent to the trade discount series 32%, 10%, 5%.

6. A retailer can buy an oak, jewelry storage chest with a list price of $170 at trade discounts of 25%, 15%, and 15%. Find the single discount that is equivalent to this discount series using the complement method, to the nearest hundredth percent.

7. A series discount of 20%, 12%, and 8% is offered on work shoes that list for $95. **a.** What percent of the list price is the invoice price? **b.** What is the single discount equivalent to the series discount? **c.** What is the invoice price of the work shoes?

Lesson 12.4 *Markup and Markdown*

Exercises

1. As the buyer for Rezden Electronics, you are buying a travel alarm clock for a line that sells at $11.98. What is the most that you can pay for the clock and maintain a markup of 45% of the selling price?

2. Your store sells two-way radio sets in two price lines. An inexpensive two-way radio set sells for $59.50. A better radio set with more features sells for $115. What is the highest cost price you can pay for each of these lines and make a markup of 48% of the selling price: **a.** the inexpensive radio set? **b.** the better radio set?

3. You must buy binoculars for a line that sells for $64.89. What is the most that you can pay for the binoculars and make a markup of 34% on the selling price?

4. A retailer paid $2.50 for a 25-foot measuring tape. What is the selling price of the measuring tape with a markup of 60% on selling price?

5. The cost price of a bag of rice is $1.10. What is the selling price of the rice if a storeowner wants a markup of 24% on selling price?

6. A retailer wants a markup of 70% of the selling price on a stainless steel thermos bottle that costs $4.80. **a.** What is the bottle's selling price? **b.** What is the amount of markup?

7. Madison Village Hardware buys a line of faucets at $80 each, less 20% and 10%. The store sells them at $90. **a.** How much does the store's markup each? **b.** What percent is this of the selling price?

Lesson 12.4 *Markup and Markdown*

8. The cost of a remote-control racer is $47.80. A retailer wants to sell the racer for $83.65. What rate of markup based on cost will the retailer use?

9. A retailer paid $18.10 for a fishing reel that is to be sold for $32.58. What rate of markup based on cost must the retailer apply to the cost price?

10. A set of cookware that costs $192.50 sells for $296.45 at a store that bases markup on cost. **a.** What is the amount of markup? **b.** What is the rate of markup on cost?

11. Early shoppers who come to a store before 8:00 a.m. get a 15% discount on all clothing. **a.** For a jacket marked at $59, what discount will an early shopper get? **b.** What is the jacket's selling price after the discount is taken?

Lesson 12.4 *Markup and Markdown*

12. On a special shopping day, a store's charge account customers get an extra 20% off on purchases of household items. The price of blankets with a marked price of $35 will be reduced by a 15% discount taken at the register. **a.** What is the blanket's reduced price, after the markdown? **a.** What is the blanket's selling price to a charge account customer?

13. To entice customers, a store advertises 20 discontinued models of inkjet printers for $29 each. The last marked price of the printers was $97. **a.** What amount of discount from the marked price was being offered? **b.** To the nearest percent, what was the rate of markdown?

14. Cronin Auto Parts bought a mechanic's tool set for $175 each, less 40%. Cronin marked the tool set to sell at $200. At a sale, the tool set was sold for 20% off the marked price. **a.** What was the invoice price of the tool set? **b.** What was the sale price? **c.** On each set sold at the sale, what was the amount the store made as markup? **d.** The markup was equal to what percent of the selling price, rounded to the nearest percent?

15. The One-Stop Building Supply Company bought 40 ladders at $49.50. One-Stop wants to sell the ladders at a 40% markup based on selling price. Thirty of the ladders were sold at the original selling price. The remaining ladders were sold after the original selling price was marked down 20%. **a.** What was the original selling price of the ladders? **b.** What was the selling price after the markdown? **c.** What was the total amount One-Stop received from the sale of the 40 ladders?

Lesson 12.5 *Marketing Surveys*

Exercises

1. A survey was mailed to 10,500 households by the city library. Of the 1,683 surveys returned, 108 were incomplete and could not be processed. What was the response rate to the survey?

2. A research firm doing telephone surveys considers surveys to be complete only if all questions are answered. Of the 580 persons in the survey population, 120 people did not answer their phone, 200 refused to answer any questions, 65 would not answer demographic questions, and 12 hung up the phone during the survey because the survey was taking too much time. All other surveys were complete. Find the survey's response rate, to the nearest tenth percent.

3. A magazine mailed 140,000 copies to subscribers. The magazine included a tear-out questionnaire and a business reply envelope to survey subscribers about a new magazine feature. Replies were received from 3,474 subscribers that included 16 envelopes with no surveys enclosed. What was the response rate to the survey, to the nearest tenth percent?

4. Run-Rite Software Company surveyed 2,000 registered buyers of TrackGen, a family-tree software product. Those surveyed were to rate three product features. Use the results shown in the following table to answer these questions: **a.** Which product feature received the most poor ratings? **b.** Of the ratings in the good category, which product feature received the highest rating? **c.** What percent of those surveyed did not use the help search feature?

Feature Rated	Feature Ratings			
	Poor	Average	Good	Don't Use
Help Menus	39	1,365	510	86
Help Search	580	1,075	133	212
Screen Customizing	72	345	1,184	399

5. A college student surveyed eyeglass wearers in a shopping mall to determine why they don't use contact lenses. Interpret the survey data shown and find: **a.** the percent of males who think that contact lens care requires too much time; **b.** the percent of females and males concerned about the expense of contact lens wear, to the nearest percent.

Reasons for Not Using Contact Lenses	Respondents	
	Female	Male
Preference (tried and didn't like)	60	40
Time (lens care requires too much time)	100	120
Expense (costly supplies are needed)	180	50
Vision (may not see as well)	60	90

     Chapter 12 *Workbook*

Lesson 12.6 *Sales Forecasts*

Exercises

1. Value Unlimited sold 4,670 restaurant discount books at a stall in a shopping mall during last year's holiday season. This year they expect to sell 20% more books because of a better location. How many books does Value Unlimited expect to sell at the mall this year?

2. Based on a long-range weather forecast predicting a colder winter and above-average snowfall, Basil Footwear expects to sell 15% more pairs of boots this year than the 340 sold last year. How many pairs of boots does Basil expect to sell this year?

3. A children's book, Jonathon's Family, sold 380 copies in a test market. The publisher decides to sell the book nationally in 72 similar markets. If the book sells at the same rate nationally as it did in the test market, how many copies should the publisher expect to sell?

4. A consumer survey showed that demand for reduced-fat snacks will increase 4.5% next year. A snack manufacturer sold 320,000 boxes of low-fat cookies last year. How many boxes of low-fat cookies can the manufacturer expect to sell next year if the survey results are accurate?

5. A sales manager expects sales of business software products to small businesses to increase 22% next year from this year's sales of $368,000. Software sales to medium-sized businesses are expected to increase 15% next year from sales of $915,000 this year. What total software sales can be expected to both types of businesses based on the sales manager's projections?

6. The executives of a pharmaceutical company expect sales of a cholesterol-lowering drug to increase 35% next year from $90,000,000 in sales this year. **a.** By how much are sales expected to increase next year? **b.** What total sales are expected?

Lesson 12.7 *Market Share*

Exercises

1. The four landscaping companies in a city had estimated total annual sales of $1,040,000 last year. One of the companies, Logan's Pebbles and Stuff, had estimated sales of $312,000 last year. What was Logan's market share, based on these estimates?

2. The sales of coffee makers are projected to be 1.5 million units next year. If Halley Manufacturing meets its goal to sell 390,000 coffee makers next year, what will be its market share?

3. The KTR Company had sales last year of $540,000 out of total industry sales of $61,000,000. Even though industry sales are not expected to increase this year, KTR expects to promote aggressively its products and gain $50,000 in additional sales each month by taking sales from competitors. **a.** What total sales does KTR expect to have this year?   Calculate KTR's market share, to the nearest tenth percent: **b.** for last year; **c.** for this year, assuming it makes the sales gains it wants.

4. Valdivia Uniform Company is estimated to have a 21% share of the $850,000 commercial uniform market in a county. What is Valdivia's market share in dollars?

5. Dillon Paving usually gets contracts for 2.5% of the $60,000,000 spent annually for street paving in a three-county area. After buying another paving business, Dillon expects to gain an additional 1.25% of street paving market share. What is Dillon's expected market share in dollars?

6. Water Experts estimates it installs 23% of the 3,200 lawn-watering systems installed each year in its market area. What is Water Experts' market share, in systems installed each year?

7. Gayle Barnett has a contract to photograph graduates at 16 of the 87 high schools in a three-county area. The average number of graduates at each high school is 230. **a.** What is the total market of graduates in the three-county area? **b.** How many graduates might Gayle expect to photograph? **c.** What is Gayle's market share, to the nearest percent?

Lesson 12.8 *Advertising*

Exercises

1. A furniture retailer is having a clearance sale and plans to run a full-page ad on Monday, Wednesday, and Friday of one week. The rate card on page 541 of the textbook lists the rates the retailer will be charged. **a.** What will be the total cost of the ads, using the base price? **b.** How much more would be spent for the ads if they were two-color ads?

2. The local zoo has a new exhibit that it wants to advertise in the regional edition of a national magazine. The four-color ad costs $156,000 if placed in all editions and $31,000 if placed in one regional edition. As a non-profit organization, the zoo receives a 12% discount from regular rates. What is the cost to the zoo of running the ad once in a regional edition?

3. A local cable operator offers banner ads on its cable channel guide. A basic package is offered to run one, 30-second ad every four hours throughout the day at a cost of $560 a day. A prime-time package will run six 30-second ads, one every 40 minutes between 6:00 p.m. and 10:00 p.m. at a cost of $810 a day. A 10% frequency discount is given for ads that run for three to seven days. If an advertiser runs cable ads for four days, what will be the total cost for: **a.** the basic package? **b.** the prime-time package? **c.** How much more per ad will it cost to advertise for four days with the prime-time package than with the basic package?

                                            Chapter 12 *Workbook*

Lesson 12.8 *Advertising*

4. A search engine charges $60,000 for a 3-month sponsor ad on its home page. A sponsor ad on a link page costs $72,000 for three months. The site averages 12,000,000 hits per month to its home page and 4,500,000 hits per month to its most popular link page. An advertiser contracts for a 3-month ad on the home page and the most-popular link page. **a.** What is the advertiser's total 3-month cost for both pages? Over the 3-month contract, what is the per-hit cost, to the nearest thousandth cent, of the: **b.** home page ad? **c.** link page ad?

5. A local retailer runs a newspaper display ad 48 times a year. The ad's usual size is 10 column inches by 6 column widths at a rate of $135 per column inch. The newspaper has a circulation of 450,000 copies and a readership of 630,000 copies. **a.** What is the usual cost of one ad? **b.** What is the cost of one ad stated as a cost per paper circulated?   **c.** What is the cost on one ad stated as a cost per reader, rounded to the nearest tenth of a cent? **d.** What is the total spent by the retailer on display ads in a year?

6. A company spent $4,800,000 in advertising on a televised sports event. This is 20% more than was spent last year. An estimated 35,000,000 people watched the telecast. What was the ad's cost per viewer, to the nearest cent?

Term Puzzler

Complete the crossword puzzle below. Some answers are two words placed together without space between them.

Across

1. Price reduction for cash payment
3. Discount from marked price
4. Part of total market a company has
6. Catalog price
9. Sale on credit
10. Reports value of returned merchandise
13. People who see or hear ad
14. Printing read by a scanner

Down

1. Difference between 100% and rate of discount
2. What a steady sales increase is called.
3. Total group to which product may be sold
5. Person answering survey
7. Balance register tally with cash on hand
8. Calculation of sales in future
11. Goods delivered to buyer are listed here
12. Covers expenses and profit

Integrated Project 12

Directions Read through the entire project before you begin doing any work.

True-Fit Manufacturing produces and sells office workstations and related furniture through authorized dealers. As a trainee with the company you will work on several projects to give you an overview of the company's operations.

Step One

Complete the following sales invoice. Apply the usual trade discount series of 30%, 15%, and 10% to the list price of each item to calculate the unit price. Do the extensions and find the invoice total. Write the last cash discount date in the space provided. Calculate the amount of cash discount based only on the invoice total. Cash discounts are not given on shipping charges of $410. List prices for workstation components follow:

Workstation w/peninsula	$980	Door, open shelf unit	$140	Task chair	$280
Open shelf unit	$260	Keyboard tray	$50		

True-Fit Manufacturing			Invoice:3-119-78	
1311 E. Bedford Road				
Raleigh, NC 27604-3441				
			Date:06/20/20--	
Sold to:Calder Office Furnishings			Ship Via:Our Truck	
4571 Sundance Parkway			Terms:2/10, n/30	
Richmond, VA 23228-1910			FOB:Raleigh	

Quantity	Stock No.	Description	Unit Price	Total
6	208-13-765	Workstation with right-hand peninsula		
6	208-15-201	Open shelf unit		
3	208-16-181	Doors, open shelf unit		
6	489-31-283	Keyboard tray		
6	ETC-16-1892	Task chair		
		Invoice Total		
1	TRK-15	Shipping		
		Total Due		
		Last date for cash discount		
		Cash discount if paid by discount date		

Integrated Project 12, continued

Step Two

Enter the total due for Invoice #3-119-78 into the customer account for Calder Office Furnishings. Note that the account balances have not been calculated after each transaction this month. Update the balance column. Other transactions will be posted to the customer account later in the project.

Account:	Calder Office Furnishings			Account No.: 11-23-823
	4571 Sundance Parkway			
	Richmond, VA 23228-1910			

Date	Description	Charges	Credits	Balance
6/1	Balance Forward			18,891.01
6/4	Payment, Invoice 3-119-76		12,871.54	
6/10	Payment, Invoice 3-119-77		4,003.30	
6/10	Cash Discount, Invoice 3-119-77		81.70	
6/20				
6/23				
6/30				
6/30				

Step Three

On June 23, Calder notifies True-Fit that the casters on two task chairs were broken. Replacement casters will be sent at no cost and Calder will be given a $15 credit per chair to cover the expense of replacing the casters. Complete the following credit memo. Record the credit memo in Calder's customer account.

Credit Memo		
True-Fit Manufacturing		
1311 E. Bedford Road		
Raleigh, NC 27604-3441		
To: Calder Office Furnishings	Account No.:	
4571 Sundance Parkway	Date:	
Richmond, VA 23228-1910	Credit Memo:	478
We have credited your account as follows:		
Description	**Unit Price**	**Total**
Total Credit		

Chapter 12 Workbook

Integrated Project 12, continued

Step Four

Payment for Invoice 3-119-78 was received from Calder on June 30 less the credit and cash discount. Record the payment in Calder's customer account. Study the customer account to see how a cash discount was recorded on June 10 to determine how to record the cash discount on June 30.

Step Five

True-Fit has excess furniture in stock that it needs to sell to make space for new stock being produced. True-Fit offers the excess furniture to dealers at the usual discount series plus another 10%.

   1. What is the single discount equivalent to the usual discount series of 30%, 15%, and 10%?

   2. What single discount equivalent will be given on excess furniture sales?

   3. A single pedestal desk whose list price is $740 is declared excess stock. **a.** What would its unit cost to dealers at the usual series discount have been? **b.** What will its unit cost at the excess furniture series discount be?

Step Six

True-Fit Manufacturing regularly assesses its marketing efforts. Provide answers to the following questions:

   4. True-Fit surveyed its 80 dealers regarding a proposal to provide direct delivery to a customer site instead of a dealer's warehouse. This would save handling costs for the dealer. True-Fit proposes to charge 2% of the invoice total for making direct deliveries with a $350 minimum delivery charge. The survey results showed that 15% of the dealers might use the service. 25% believe the proposed delivery charge is too high and should be 1% of invoice with a $100 minimum, and 60% would not use the service. Based on the data provided, should True-Fit offer direct delivery at its proposed terms? Give reasons for your answer.

Integrated Project 12, continued

5. True-Fit has annual sales of about $18 million. The sales manager projects that hiring two salespersons at a total cost of $156,000 a year would increase sales by 5%. Assume that two salespersons are hired and the sales manager's projection is correct. What total sales might True-Fit expect next year if all other factors affecting sales remain the same?

6. True-Fit's Vice-President of Finance believes that there might be a general business slowdown next year and that sales may drop as much as 6%. All expenses will be considered for possible cutbacks. True-Fit spends about $5,000 a month on advertising to small businesses that are the primary buyers of True-Fit products from dealers. Another advertising expense is a $1,200 annual payment given to each dealer to support the dealer's efforts to promote the True-Fit brand. **a.** If all advertising were eliminated for one year, how much would True-Fit save? **b.** Should all advertising be eliminated to save money?

Chapter 12 Workbook

Lesson 13.1 *Preparing Income Statements*

Exercises

1. For the last quarter, the total sales of Prime Discount, Inc. were $183,782.15. The sales returns and allowances for the month totaled $8,452.97. What were the shop's net sales for the month?

2. Gene's Auto Supply had total sales of $326,868.53 for the month. Sales returns and allowances for the month totaled $27,840.63. What were the net sales?

3. A store calculates its cost of goods sold every quarter. On July 1, the store's goods inventory was $386,700. Purchases during the quarter were $485,929. The ending inventory on September 30 was $423,745. For the three months, what was the cost of goods available for sale? What was the cost of goods sold?

4. On March 1, the beginning inventory of Yancy Manufacturing Company was $688,145. During the month, Yancy produced goods costing $905,331. The inventory at the end of March was $745,198. Find Yancy's cost of goods sold for March.

5. Sinclair Outdoor Equipment Company had net sales of $302,877 for the first quarter of the year. During the same period, its cost of goods sold was $181,279. Find the company's gross profit for the quarter.

6. Triand Office Supply Company had total sales of $86,940.23 for the month. Sales returns and allowances totaled $3,210.75. The cost of the goods sold during the month was $42,922.80. What were Triand's net sales? What was the company's gross profit on sales?

Lesson 13.1 *Preparing Income Statements*

7. A pharmacy had net sales of $835,000 for March. The cost of goods sold during the month was $591,350, and the operating expenses were $204,500. Find the gross profit on sales for March. Find the net income for the month.

8. In April, the gross profit on sales for a children's toy store was $54,387. Operating expenses for the month totaled $58,895. For the month, what was the store's net loss? If the amount of the monthly loss continues at the same rate for the whole year, how much will the store lose?

9. The Gesteral Appliance Company gives you these data for their March operations: net sales, $246,495; inventory at beginning of month, $54,740; purchases during the month, $154,250; inventory at end of month, $59,160; operating expenses, $78,325. Write these figures in the correct spaces of the form below and show the **a.** cost of goods sold, **b.** gross profit on sales, **c.** net income or loss. Use a minus sign to show a net loss.

GESTERAL APPLIANCE COMPANY

Net Sales	_________	
Less Cost of Goods Sold:		
Inventory, March 1	_________	
Add Purchases	_________	
Goods Available for Sale	_________	
Less Inventory, March 31	_________	
Cost of Goods Sold		a. _________
Gross Profit on Sales		b. _________
Less Operating Expenses	_________	
Net Income or Loss		c. _________________

    Chapter 13 *Workbook*

Lesson 13.2 *Analyzing Income Statements*

Exercises

1. The summaries of two income statements follow. For each statement, find what percent each item in the statement is of the net sales.

Income Statement A			Income Statement B		
Major Items	Amount	Percent	Major Items	Amount	Percent
Net Sales	$300,000	**a.**	Net Sales	$64,000	**f.**
Cost of Goods Sold	180,000	**b.**	Cost of Goods Sold	28,800	**g.**
Gross Profit on Sales	$120,000	**c.**	Gross Profit on Sales	$35,200	**h.**
Operating Expenses	90,000	**d.**	Operating Expenses	30,080	**i.**
Net Income	$ 30,000	**e.**	Net Income	$ 5,120	**j.**

2. During March, a music store had net sales of $270,000. The gross profit was $121,500 and the operating expenses were $108,000. As a percent of net sales, what was the gross profit margin? What was the net income for March? What was the net profit margin?

3. During a quarter, a storeowner made a gross profit of $162,000 on net sales of $360,000. The operating expenses for the period were $144,000. What was the net income for the quarter? As a percent of net sales, what was the gross profit margin? What was the net profit margin?

4. Last year, The Preston Art Supply Store's merchandise inventory on January 1 was $42,300; on July 1, $51,500; on December 31, $44,800. The cost of goods sold during the year was $173,200. What was the merchandise turnover rate for the year to two decimal places?

5. Braniff Electronics' cost of goods sold during October was $144,900. The merchandise inventory on October 1 was $187,500 and on October 31 it was $174,300. What was the store's turnover rate to the nearest tenth percent for the month?

Lesson 13.3 *Partnership Income*

Exercises

1. Geraint invests $184,000 and Ammah invests $276,000 in a partnership they form. If they have no written partnership agreement, what would be each partner's share of a $127,880 profit? If they agree to share profits and losses in proportion to their investments, what amount would be Geraint's share of a $35,880 loss and what would be Ammah's share?

2. Three partners have these investments in a small bakery: Sabatini, $84,000; Stein, $105,000; and Clark, $63,000. The business makes a profit of $134,400. The partners agree to share profits in proportion to their investment. What is Sabatini's share of the profit? What is Stein's share of the profit? What is Clark's share?

3. Hakim and Washington are partners in a hardware outlet. Their partnership agreement shows that net income is to be shared in the ratio of 7 to 5 in favor of Hakim. **a.** If their business produces a net income of $394,320, what amount will be Hakim's share? **b.** What amount will be Washington's share?

4. O'Malley and Schmidt are business partners who divide their net income as follows: 52% to O'Malley and 48% to Schmidt. Of a net income of $369,820, what amount is O'Malley's share? What amount is Schmidt's share?

Lesson 13.3 *Partnership Income*

5. In the partnership of Lee and Liang, a net income of $114,495 for one year is divided between the partners in a ratio of 8 to 7. Lee is given 8 parts and Liang is given 7 parts. What is Lee's share of the net income? What is Liang's share?

6. Ai-Lien Ho and Sandy Roth are partners in a business with investments of $360,000 and $60,000, respectively. Their agreement states that net income is to be divided by paying the partners 12% interest annually on their investments and dividing the rest equally. At the end of one year, the net income is $89,700. In the table below, you are to show the interest both partners receive on their investments and their share of the remaining income. Then show the total income received by both and the totals of all three columns.

Partner	Interest on Investment	Share of Remaining Income	Total Share of Net Income
Ai-Lien Ho			
Sandy Roth			
Totals			

7. Three partners in a kitchen-remodeling firm invested these amounts: Loeb, $56,000; Martinez, $42,000; Wilson, $28,000. Their agreement provides that each will receive 8% interest on their investment with any remaining income to be distributed in proportion to their investments. If the total net income for a year is $235,620, find the share each partner will get, rounded to the nearest dollar.

Lesson 13.4 *Preparing Balance Sheets*

Exercises

1. Daryn Brown owns a pet supply store. The store has assets valued at $209,872 and liabilities of $73,307. How much is Daryn's capital?

2. Myrleen Shanders owns a beauty salon. On January 1 she has these items in the business: cash of $1,760, merchandise worth $4,824, store supplies worth $635, and store equipment valued at $11,147. She owes the R&E Supply Company $1,386, and Telride Equipment, Inc. $3,163. (a) What is the total amount of Myrleen's assets? What is the total of her liabilities? What is the amount of her capital?

3. Tomas Nieves owns a small business with these assets: cash, $2,479; merchandise inventory, $45,124; store supplies, $1,647; store equipment, $21,872; land and building, $172,500. He owes T-Bar, Inc. $7,875, American Supply, Inc. $6,280, and United Savings and Loan $101,795. (a) Find his total assets. Find his total liabilities. Find the amount of his capital.

4. At the end of the year, Suba Ahtma, owner of Eastern Gifts, made a balance sheet. You are to complete this balance sheet by showing the total assets, the total liabilities, the capital, and the total liabilities and capital.

EASTERN GIFTS
Balance Sheet, December 31, 20–

Assets		Liabilities	
Cash	$3,567.54	Genesco Merchandise Co.	$10,697.62
Accounts Receivable	478.00	Lianda Crafts	11,582.53
Merchandise Inventory	54,853.50	First National Bank	8,150.00
Store Supplies	1,945.00	Total Liabilities	__________
Store Equipment	9,237.00		
Office Equipment	4,107.00	**Capital**	
Other Assets	6,954.85	Marisa Dressner, Capital	__________
Total Assets	__________	Total Liabilities and Capital	__________

Lesson 13.5 *Analyzing Balance Sheets*

Exercises

1. A bookstore has $218,710 in current liabilities and $348,160 in current assets. What is the store's current ratio, to the nearest tenth?

2. The balance sheet of Cordoba Wholesalers, Inc. shows $2,285,320 in current liabilities and $4,248,530 in current assets. What is its current ratio, to the nearest tenth?

3. An electronic store has these assets: cash, $5,180; accounts receivable, $4,820; merchandise inventory, $168,110; store supplies, $8,170; store equipment, $22,800; delivery equipment, $47,200. It has the following liabilities: accounts payable, $75,160, a 30-day promissory note to a supplier for $8,500, and 3-year loans on delivery equipment for $25,070. What is the store's current ratio, to the nearest tenth?

4. Fifth Street Bistro has long-term debts of $46,920 and capital of $78,450. Find its debt-to-equity ratio, shown as a percent to the nearest tenth.

5. Pentane Movies, Inc. has a mortgage on its theater for $245,700 and a 2-year bank loan for $125,000. Pentane's total capital is $854,500. Find its debt-to-equity ratio, shown as a percent to the nearest tenth.

6. Ferocity Car Washes, Inc. showed a net income of $127,840 on its December 31 income statement. The balance sheet on the same day showed capital of $212,950. Find its return on equity, to the nearest tenth percent.

7. Tonne Sales Corporation's income statement showed these amounts on December 31: net sales, $1,263,336; cost of goods sold, $755,650; and operating expenses of $315,800. Its balance sheet showed capital of $1,226,400. Find its return on equity, to the nearest tenth percent.

Lesson 13.6 *Bankruptcy*

Exercises

1. Rod Aaron owns a mailing and shipping store. He is unable pay the debts of the store and has been forced into bankruptcy. After selling the assets and paying the bankruptcy costs, the trustee has cash to pay creditors 28% of their claims. If Aaron owes the C-Packaging, Inc. $12,580, how much should that company receive? Another company, Trenton Cartons, Inc., has a claim against Aaron for $6,340. How much should Trenton Cartons, Inc. receive?

2. Campus Computer Corporation has debts of $360,000. The store declares bankruptcy and its assets are sold. After bankruptcy costs are paid, $154,800 is left to pay creditor claims. What percent can the trustee pay of the creditor claims? How much will J-Tech Supply Company, with a claim of $5,076, get?

3. The Cone Shop declares bankruptcy with debts of $72,000. After bankruptcy costs are paid, the trustee has only $21,600 for payment to creditors. To settle their claims, how much on the dollar will the creditors be paid? How much will a creditor with a claim of $885 be paid?

4. The Sea Shell Gift Shop was declared bankrupt. After selling the company's assets for $16,760, the trustee paid $9,200 for bankruptcy fees and paid creditor claims of $50,400 with the rest of the money. What amount was left to pay creditor claims? What percent of claims did each creditor get? Beamis Supply Company, one of the creditors, had a claim for $3,200. How much were they paid?

5. When Kline Landscape Design was declared bankrupt, it owed its creditors $218,750. A trustee sold the assets for $65,544.75. From this money, the trustee must first pay court costs and other bankruptcy charges totaling $15,221.25. Creditors of Kline will be paid from the remaining money. What is the total amount available to pay creditor claims? What is the total amount of their claims that the creditors will lose? How much on the dollar will each creditor will receive?

Term Puzzler

Directions Some of the words listed below are in the puzzle. Circle each term when you find it. It may be written downward, upward, sideways, or diagonally. There are 18 terms in the puzzle. How many can you find?

Accounts receivable	Debt-to-equity ratio	Net loss
Assets	Ending inventory	Net profit margin
Balance sheet	Gross profit	Net income
Bankrupt	Gross profit margin	Net sales
Capital	Income statement	Operating expenses
Cost of goods sold	Liabilities	Partnership
Creditors	Long-term liabilities	Return on Equity
Current Ratio	Merchandise turnover rate	Revenue

```
C  U  R  R  E  N  T  R  A  T  I  O  P  Q  O  N  R
O  A  S  S  E  T  S  I  B  A  N  K  R  U  P  T  G
S  M  P  W  P  V  B  Q  C  Y  G  O  D  C  A  O  I
T  Q  U  I  M  N  E  T  I  N  C  O  M  E  R  I  N
O  P  R  E  T  U  R  N  O  N  E  Q  U  I  T  Y  C
F  K  I  X  S  A  K  K  U  R  R  T  E  P  N  V  O
G  I  G  K  R  E  L  Q  S  E  K  N  L  Q  E  Y  M
O  E  N  D  I  N  G  I  N  V  E  N  T  O  R  Y  E
O  P  E  R  A  T  I  N  G  E  X  P  E  N  S  E  S
D  K  T  K  K  C  L  S  M  M  V  B  D  V  H  S  T
S  D  S  J  B  G  R  O  S  S  P  R  O  F  I  T  A
S  B  A  L  A  N  C  E  S  H  E  E  T  T  P  O  T
O  Q  L  V  Q  B  V  E  D  D  V  I  P  L  D  D  E
L  M  E  S  E  I  T  I  L  I  B  A  I  L  E  H  M
D  Y  S  H  A  D  D  T  C  Q  T  R  C  D  N  F  E
J  H  N  G  G  V  Q  R  W  O  T  O  Q  F  Y  L  N
I  L  X  Z  N  N  S  U  V  J  X  B  R  U  X  C  T
F  M  Q  E  N  C  F  M  C  H  J  W  K  S  E  K  B
```

Integrated Project 13

Directions Read through the entire project before you begin doing any work.

Introduction A partially completed annual income statement and balance sheet for the Transita Company follow. Transita was formed by three partners who invested these amounts of money in the business: John Lee, $80,000; Ana Salazar, $100,000; Rita Vitale, $120,000. The business owns a lot and building on which the partners have a 25-year mortgage with First Bank. The building contains an office and warehouse.

Their partnership agreement specifies that partners be paid 8% interest on their investments in the business with any remaining net income to be divided this way: 30% to Lee, 30% to Salazar, and 40% to Vitale.

Transita Company Income Statement, For the Year Ended December 31, 20--				
			Percent	
			Analysis	
Sales	526,800			
Less Sales Returns and Allowances	15,809			
Net Sales				
Cost of Merchandise Sold				
Merchandise Inventory, January 1	54,600			
Purchases	267,800			
Merchandise Available for Sale	322,400			
Less Merchandise Inventory, December 31	48,930			
Cost of Goods Sold				
Gross Profit on Sales				
Operating Expenses				
Employee Wages	45,627			
Mortgage Interest	12,537			
Taxes	12,850			
Utilities	8,213			
Advertising	8,987			
Depreciation of Equipment	8,470			
Depreciation of Building	7,950			
Depreciation of Trucks	7,425			
Truck Repair and Maintenance	4,530			
Insurance	13,100			
Other Expenses	7,250			
Total Operating Expenses				
Net Income				

Integrated Project 13, *continued*

<table>
<tr><td colspan="4" align="center">Transita Company</td></tr>
<tr><td colspan="4" align="center">Balance Sheet, December 31, 20—</td></tr>
<tr><td colspan="4"></td></tr>
<tr><td align="center">Assets</td><td></td><td align="center">Liabilities</td><td></td></tr>
<tr><td>Cash</td><td>$51,670</td><td>A-1 Supply Company</td><td>$15,210</td></tr>
<tr><td>Accounts Receivable</td><td>44,342</td><td>Reliable Supplies, Inc.</td><td>4,537</td></tr>
<tr><td>Office Supplies</td><td>3,775</td><td>First Bank</td><td>180,345</td></tr>
<tr><td>Merchandise Inventory</td><td>48,930</td><td align="center">Total Liabilities</td><td></td></tr>
<tr><td>Office Equipment</td><td>34,740</td><td align="center">Capital</td><td></td></tr>
<tr><td>Warehouse Equipment</td><td>44,360</td><td>John Lee, Capital</td><td>$ 80,000</td></tr>
<tr><td>Delivery Trucks</td><td>37,125</td><td>Ana Salazar, Capital</td><td>100,000</td></tr>
<tr><td>Land and Buildings</td><td>235,150</td><td>Rita Vitale, Capital</td><td>120,000</td></tr>
<tr><td></td><td></td><td align="center">Total Capital</td><td></td></tr>
<tr><td>Total Assets</td><td></td><td>Total Liabilities and Capital</td><td></td></tr>
</table>

Step One

Fill in the missing amounts and percentages on the income statement and the missing amounts on the balance sheet. Round percentages to the nearest whole percent. Then complete the following exercises.

1. On the average, what was the amount of net income that Transita earned each month?

2. Find the merchandise turnover rate for the year, correct to two decimal places.

3. **a.** What was the total of Transita's current assets on December 31? **b.** What were Transita's total current liabilities?

4. What was Transita's current ratio, to the nearest tenth?

5. What was Transita's debt-to-equity ratio, to the nearest tenth percent?

Integrated Project 13, continued

6. What was Transita's return on equity, to the nearest tenth percent?

Step Two

Complete the following table by figuring each partner's share of net income under the current partnership agreement.

TRANSITA COMPANY
Distribution of Net Income to Partners

Partner	Interest on Investment	Share of Total Amount Remaining Net Income	Received
Lee, John	________	________	________
Salazar, Ana	________	________	________
Vitale, Rita	________	________	________
Total	________	________	________

Step Three

After repeated calls and letters to a customer requesting payment of a $3,500 overdue account, Transita received a letter from the customer's bankruptcy trustee. The letter indicated that the customer had $124,500 in debts, far fewer assets, and was forced to declare bankruptcy.

After selling the customer's assets and subtracting legal costs, the amount remaining for creditors was $28,340. **a.** Find the percent that creditors will receive on their claims, to the nearest tenth of a percent. **b.** Find the cents on the dollar received by creditors, to the nearest tenth of a cent. **c.** Find the amount. Transita will receive on its overdue account.

   Name ____ Date ____________

Lesson 14.1 *Production, Trade, and Finance*

Exercises

Find the per capita Gross Domestic Product (GDP) for each country listed, to the nearest dollar.

	Country	Population	Gross Domestic Product	Per Capita GDP
1.	Australia	20,090,000	$612 billion	
2.	Cambodia	13,600,000	$27 billion	
3.	Cuba	11,350,000	$34 billion	
4.	France	60,700,000	$1.74 trillion	
5.	India	1,080,000,000	$3.32 trillion	

6. Recently, Fiji had imports of $838 million and exports of $655 million. Did Fiji have a trade deficit or surplus, and how much?

7. The United States' exports to Brazil were $13.202 billion and its imports from Brazil were $11.313 billion. Did the U.S. have a trade deficit or surplus with Brazil? What was the amount?

Lesson 14.1 *Production, Trade, and Finance*

8. In a recent year, Canada has imports of $202,700,000,000 and exports of $210,700,000,000. **a.** Did Canada have a trade deficit or surplus? **b.** How much was the deficit or surplus? **c.** About 80% of Canada's exports were to the U.S. What was the value of these exports, to the nearest hundred million dollars?

9. The value of Hong Kong's dollar (HK$) in U.S. dollars is $0.1285. A designer gown costs 15,000 HK$. What is the equivalent value in U.S. dollars?

10. A Russian ruble is valued at $0.03416 in U.S. dollars. What is the equivalent cost in U.S. dollars of a hotel room in Moscow with a nightly rate of 2,400 rubles, to the nearest dollar?

11. Brazil's national currency is the real (R). There are 2.8540 R in a U.S. dollar. You filled a rental car in Brazil with 45 L of gasoline at a cost of 92 R. How much did you pay in U.S. dollars?

12. In Indonesia's currency, there are 9,453 rupiah in one U.S. dollar. The value of a claim to a tin mine is 2,500,000 rupiah. What is the claim's value in U.S. dollars, to the nearest ten dollars?

                                                  Chapter 14 *Workbook*

Lesson 14.2 *International Time and Temperature*

Exercises

1. It is 8:00 P.M. in Chicago, Illinois. What time is it in the following cities? Use the time zone chart on page 598 of the textbook.

   a. Washington, D. C.

   b. Khartoum, Africa

   c. Lima, Peru

   d. Paris, France

   e. Tokyo, Japan

2. It is 6:00 A.M. on Wednesday, March 15 in Manila, Philippines. What day, date, and time is it in Denver, Colorado?

3. You are eating lunch at 12:30 P.M. in New York City, NY on Sunday, January 31. What are the day, date, and time in Shanghai, China?

4. A business traveler who is in Casablanca, Morocco telephones the home office in Perth, Australia at 2:00 A.M. on Tuesday, November 12. At what day, date, and time was the call answered?

5. Show the equivalent Celsius or Fahrenheit temperature for each of the following, to the nearest tenth degree:

   a.   320°F

   b.   100°C

   c.   45°F

   d.   68°C

   e.   −15°F

Lesson 14.3 *International Measures of Length*

Exercises

1. Armand Ritter is building a storage unit to hold his DVD collection. Each DVD is about 20 mm wide. How many centimeters wide must a shelf be to hold 3-dozen DVDs?

2. Plastic tubing 8 meters long was cut into 5 equal pieces. What was the length of each piece: **a.** in meters? **b.** in centimeters? **c.** in millimeters?

3. A boat supply store, George's Marine Sales and Service, placed on sale a 600-meter roll of nylon rope. These lengths of rope were sold from the roll: 33 m, 70 m, 100 m, 150 m, 14 m, and 40 m. **a.** How many meters of rope were sold from the roll? **b.** How many meters of rope were left on the roll?

4. A private pilot flew these distances in five trips: 163 km, 257 km, 218 km, 450 km, and 92 km. **a.** How many kilometers did the pilot fly in five trips? **b.** What was the average distance flown per trip, in kilometers? **c.** What equivalent distance in miles did the pilot fly on these five trips?

5. A local safety club bought reflective tape for the safety helmets of 90 children at a local school. They figure that each helmet needs these amounts and lengths of tapes: 2 strips, each 24 cm long; 4 strips, each 16 cm long. **a.** How many centimeters of tape are needed for each helmet? **b.** How many meters of tape are needed for 90 helmets?

6. A baby was 51.5 cm long at birth. At six months, the baby was 68.8 cm long. **a.** How many inches long was the baby at birth, to the nearest inch? **b.** How many centimeters did the baby grow in six months? **c.** How many inches did the baby grow in six months, to the nearest tenth inch?

     Chapter 14 *Workbook*

Lesson 14.4 *International Measures of Area*

Exercises

1. A table measures 50 cm by 115 cm. **a.** What is the table's area in square centimeters? **b.** What is the table's area in square meters?

2. A soccer stadium was built on a plot of land 200 meters × 240 meters. **a.** What area in square meters was used to build the stadium? **b.** What was the area in hectare?

3. A piece of construction paper 40 cm by 60 cm was cut into 5 equal pieces. What was the area of each piece in square centimeters and in square millimeters?

4. A land developer offered for sale 180 hectares of land. One builder bought 70.5 ha of the land to use for single-family homes. Another builder bought 87.2 ha to use for condominiums. How many hectares of land does the developer still own?

5. One wall of an office building measures 6 m by 30 m. Each of the 24 windows in the wall measures 0.8 m by 2.5 m. The rest of the wall surface is brick. **a.** What is the area of the wall in square meters? **b.** How many square meters of the wall are used for windows? **c.** How many square meters of the wall surface are brick? **d.** What is the area of the wall in square feet?

6. A farmer bought two sections of land. One section is 1 200 m by 500 m; the other is 200 m × 140 m. Wheat was planted on one half of the larger section and soybeans on the other half. The smaller section was left idle. **a.** How many hectares are in these two sections of land? **b.** How many acres are there in these two sections of land? **c.** How many hectares of land were used to grow wheat? **d.** How many hectares of land were left idle?

Lesson 14.5 *International Measures of Capacity and Weight*

Exercises

1. A bottle holds 400 milliliters of moisturizing lotion when full. What is the capacity of the bottle in liters?

2. A gas station sold 21.12 kL of gasoline in three days. **a.** What were the gas station's sales for the three days in liters? **b.** What were average daily sales in L for the three days?

3. A certain chemical is produced in a 12-liter batch. The chemical is poured into a 250 mL bottle and sold in that size. How many 250 mL bottles can be filled from one batch of the chemical?

4. A sugar-free cola can be bought in 354 mL cans or 1L bottles. **a.** If you bought a case of 24 cans, how much cola would buy in milliliters? in liters? **b.** How many one-liter bottles would you have to buy to get at least as much cola as you get in a case of 24 cans?

5. In five days, a lawn-care service used these amounts of gasoline: Monday, 23.8 liters; Tuesday, 32.7 liters; Wednesday, 16.5 liters; Thursday, 20.8 liters; Friday, 26.4 liters. **a.** How many liters of gasoline were used in these five days?   **b.** To the nearest whole gallon, how many gallons of gasoline were used in five days?

Lesson 14.5 *International Measures of Capacity and Weight*

6. Delia Burgos has to use a larger truck than she needed to deliver 75 microwave ovens. For the trip, she used 70 liters of gas. If she had used a smaller truck, she would have used 15% less gas. **a.** What amount of gas, in liters, would she have used in the smaller truck? **b.** If gas costs 1.24 euro dollars per liter, how much could she have saved by using the smaller truck? **c.** What amount of gas did she use for the delivery, in gallons?

7. A tank that holds 45,000 gallons of crude oil is 80% full. What is the amount of crude oil the tank contains measured in gallons? in kiloliters?

8. A car requires 5 quarts of new motor oil when the engine oil is changed. What is the equivalent amount of motor oil measured in liters?

9. A box of salt weighs 0.737 kilograms. What is its weight in grams?

10. The net weight of a box of pasta is 454 grams. The boxes of pasta are packed 48 boxes to a case. A factory shipped 64 cases of pasta to a distributor. **a.** What was the net weight of the box in kilograms? **b.** Excluding the weight of the containers, how many kilograms of pasta were shipped, to the nearest kilogram?

Lesson 14.5 *International Measures of Capacity and Weight*

11. Haldifor Steel Products used 400 sheets of steel to make heavy-duty shelving. Each sheet weighed 32.8 kilograms. In making the shelving, 2% of the steel used became scrap. How much did the scrap weigh in kilograms?

12. Kyle Traylor loaded this shipment of office furniture and equipment onto a truck: 24 computers, each weighing 19 kg; 24 monitors, each weighing 17 kg; 8 desks weighing 116 kg each; 15 filing cabinets weighing 46 kg each. **a.** What was the total weight of the shipment that Kyle loaded in kilograms? **b.** If the truck weighed 4 600 kg, what was the combined weight of the truck, furniture, and equipment?

13. A lawn sprinkler that used to weigh 0.65 kilograms was redesigned to make it lighter. The sprinkler now weighs 455 grams. **a.** After being redesigned, how much less did the sprinkler weigh in grams? **b.** This is what percent less than its former weight.

14. A case of paint contains 12 one-liter cans packed in a cardboard box. Each can of paint weighs 1.12 kilograms. The cardboard box weighs 520 grams. **a.** What is the total weight of the case of paint in kilograms? **b.** What is the total weight of the case of paint in pounds, to the nearest tenth of a pound?

15. A football player weighs 126 kilograms. What is the player's weight in pounds?

16. A supermarket clerk packed 80, 5-pound bags of potatoes for a weekend sale. **a.** What does each bag of potatoes weigh in kilograms? **b.** What was the total weight of the potatoes packed, in kilograms?

Term Puzzler

Complete the crossword puzzle below. Some answers are two words placed together without space between them.

Across

1. Spaced 15° of longitude apart
5. Sales to other countries
6. A country's money
7. Shows how much a container holds
9. Time zone for Boston and New York
11. Purchases from other countries
13. Located in England
14. Temperature scale used in everyday life in U.S.
17. A thousand liters

Down

2. Measuring system most often used in other countries
3. Currency created on January 1, 1999
4. Water's freezing point is 0 degrees
5. $1 = 0.3069 KD
8. Per person
10. Also known as international business
12. A centimeter measures this
15. Result of length times width
16. Popular reference to mass in U.S.

Integrated Project 14

Directions Read through the entire project before you begin doing any work.

This project provides an overview of economic statistics and items that relate to living and working in an international community.

Step One
The Bureau of Census estimates the population in the United States at 296,100,000 people and the population of the world at 6.5 billion people. The Gross Domestic Product (GDP) of the United States is estimated to be about $11.75 trillion. Other recent estimates are: U.S. exports, $795 billion; U.S. imports, $1.476 trillion. Answer the following questions based on these data.

1. What is the estimated per capita GDP of the United States, to the nearest dollar?

2. Did the U.S. have a trade surplus or deficit, and what was the amount, written as a whole number?

3. What percent of the world's population lives in the U.S., to the nearest tenth percent?

Step Two
Because of the amount of trade and other contacts made with international organizations, U.S. residents must be able to find the time of day in other countries, convert currencies, and convert customary and metric measures. Answer the following questions to test your knowledge in these areas.

4. A company has its headquarters in San Francisco and branch offices in the countries listed below. It is Monday, November 30, 11:05 a. m. PST in San Francisco. What date and time is it in:

    a. Novosibirsk, Russian Federation?

    b. Madrid, Spain?

    c. Cairo, Egypt?

    d. Hong Kong, China?

     Chapter 14 *Workbook*

Integrated Project 14, continued

5. The exchange rate between the U.S. dollar and the Japanese yen is: 1 yen = $0.009419. Find the prices in U.S. dollars for typical items sold in Japan and priced in yen as shown.

   a. Movie admission, 1,600 yen

   b. Pizza, 10-inch size: 3,000 yen

   c. Soft drink, 120 yen

6. A couple boards an airplane in Madison, Wisconsin where the temperature is 8°F. They are flying to Caracas, Venezuela where the temperature is 34°C. What is Caracas' temperature in Fahrenheit, to the nearest whole degree?

7. An ergonomics consultant suggested that the maximum weight to be lifted by hand by all employees in a shipping department is 45 lbs. A manufacturer in Taiwan wants to package cutlery sets in a box whose gross weight will be 22.3 kg. Will the shipping department employees be able to lift the boxes by hand and be within the suggested weight limit? Give a reason for your answer.

8. The state of Kentucky's area measures about 40,411 square miles. Iceland's area measures about 103 000 square kilometers. Which area is larger in whole square kilometers, Kentucky or Iceland? Give a reason for your answer.

9. Convert each of the following into the metric or customary measures, as indicated.

   a. The Hope diamond is on display at the National Gallery of Art in Washington, D. C. It weighs 45.52 carats. One carat is equal to 200 mg. What is the Hope diamond's weight in grams and ounces?

   b. The distance traveled during the first successful controlled, powered flight by Orville Wright in 1903 was 120 feet. What was the flight's distance in meters?

   c. The surface area of Lake Garda in Italy is 370 km². What is Lake Garda's approximate area in square miles, to the nearest square mile?

   d. The driving distance from Geneva, Switzerland to Vienna, Austria is 1 040 kilometers. What is the distance in miles?